Beyond Survival to VICTORY!

A Practical Guide for Victorious Christian Living

by

Leon Carter Price

Fairmont Books is a ministry of The McDougal Foundation, Inc., a Maryland nonprofit corporation dedicated to spreading the Gospel of the Lord Jesus Christ to as many people as possible in the shortest time possible. Fairmont Books, P.O. Box 3595, Hagerstown, MD 21742-3595, www.mcdougalpublishing.com.
ISBN 1-58158-039-8 (Formerly ISBN 0-9637311-0-6)
Printed in the United States of America for Worldwide Distribution

Table of Contents

FOREWORD

There are millions of sincere, dedicated Christians who go through life day by day just barely surviving in their circumstances, their activities, and their emotional lives. This is far more than just an unfortunate situation. This is a tragedy that has overtaken the nation and the Christian community.

It is *not* reasonable for this situation to continue. It *is* reasonable to recognize that there are answers and solutions available to everyone who really wants to move from a survival mode to a victorious Christian life. The Scriptures are filled with wisdom and instruction that can bring victory in every department of our lives and allow us to become what we sincerely desire to be in the purposes of God.

Although there are times that everyone is happy to find that they have emerged from a season of tragedy or great stress and have become "survivors", what may seem to be only survival is really victory over the utter defeat that could have been suffered. Mere survival is never gratifying in the long run.

We have been conditioned by the world around us to believe that survival is all we can reasonably expect from life. This is not what we are told by God's Word. This is not what the Lord Jesus said.

Jesus said that He came that we might have life, and have it more abundantly (John 10:10). The Apostle Paul says that we are more than conquerors through Him (Romans 8:37), therefore, it is not our portion to accept a life with only survival as our ultimate reward.

These are dramatic times in which we live. The Gospel is proliferating with unprecedented speed, and the so-called "developing" peoples and nations are in many instances the greatest beneficiaries of the present outpouring of God's grace. In the face of all the unrighteousness and signs of impending societal collapse all around us, we can become the victorious servants of Christ that overcome in the face of every circumstance.

Where do we start? We start with gaining victory in our own lives! In this book we want to deal with some of the practical areas where survival has frequently been considered the norm. We *can win* the victory if we *can hear* the counsel that is so available to all of us in the inscripted word.

Let us look at some of these practical areas and let the Word of God and the Holy Spirit lead us past the survival mode into a victory mode in each area. We will never be the same and our quality of life will be enhanced and improved beyond measure if we can hear what God will say to us in these chapters. We can also reach the potential to become the kind of Christians that God intends us to be. As we become victorious, we can lead others into the same overcoming life in Jesus Christ that we ourselves experience.

When we, as God's people, live in a place of victory, the Kingdom of God within us will attract and revitalize all who hear the sound of it and touch the joy of it.

INTRODUCTION

Because I was born and reared in a small town in rural Arkansas, I am familiar with the prevailing environment. This is primarily a farming area and could well be categorized as a natural arena for producing social and economic victims. However, even in this cultural climate some people emerge as victors rather than survivors.

Ross Perot came out of a one room school house in rural Arkansas and became a multi-billionaire. Sam Walton came from a small, rural Arkansas town and founded Wal-Mart, one of the world's largest retailers. Paul "Bear" Bryant rose from a rural Arkansas childhood to become a legendary football coach and hero and role model to athletes across the nation. Bill Clinton emerged from rural Arkansas to become President of the United States of America.

Somehow people in their natural environment find the determination and the perseverance to overcome obstacles and circumstances and become winners. The world is full of success stories, but what about victory for God's own people in the Church and in the Kingdom of God? Victory and joyous life reports should be the norm, not the exception. All Christians begin their walk with God with victorious hearts. We move from the kingdom of darkness into the Kingdom of Light when we take our places in the body of Christ through the blood of the Lord Jesus. As we look around us, however, we find that a great many citizens of His eternal Kingdom live only survival lives.

After "doing my own thing" as a very young man, I found entrance into His salvation and His Kingdom because of His marvelous grace. I was raised in and out of two different mainline churches without ever meeting Christ Jesus. I did not question or doubt the authenticity of the Bible. I did not doubt that Jesus died for me. I just wasn't very interested because I had other things to do. I am sure that godly men and women tried to reach out to me in my teen years, but I had other ambitions and goals that did not include spiritual pursuits. Music was my predominant interest, and I gave myself to it with everything in me.

Although I was told about Christ in my youth, I was finally arrested by the Holy Spirit only after I had played music professionally in California, served three years in the military in World War II, and returned to my career in Hollywood and other parts of the West Coast.

One day I was in Los Angeles and returned to my open, unlocked car parked at the curb. I picked up and read a gospel tract that had been thrown on the front seat. People were praying for me and the tract spoke to me. Then I retrieved a little Gideon New Testament that had been given to me in the Army, and began to read it. As the Spirit and the Word dealt with me and convicted me of my great need, I surrendered all my life to Christ and found a new victory.

My conversion was somewhat dramatic in that I felt the need to lay down my career and hopes for the worldly success that I had pursued so diligently for the first 22 years of my life. In my inner man I effectively died. The fear of God, or of missing God, was the primary dynamic in my decision to lay down the life that I knew and loved in order to enter a new life that was foreign to the man that I had been. But God met me. He also provided all that I needed to emerge from my old place into a new life where victory, righteousness, peace, and joy are always available to me.

Transition times in our lives always contain an element of apprehension because of fear of the unknown. We say, "What am I getting myself into?" But God is always faithful to meet us in our needs. He consistently helps the man or woman who will trust Him to lead them on into a place of victory.

My own numerous experiences with changes, fears, and resistance from opposing forces have provided me with insights into the ways God can and does bring victory into our live in spite of adverse circumstances. I have had the privilege of ministering to many of His precious people when survival seemed to be their greatest hope. I have also seen God meet them time after time with great victory when they have trusted and obeyed Him.

This is not a book of platitudes and untried formulas, nor a collection of hearsay regarding overcoming problems in peoples' lives. This is a book to offer practical, scriptural help toward an ongoing victorious life for sincere, dedicated Christians who have found themselves locked into a life of frustrating survivalism. There is a victory over, in, and through every circumstance. I have watched it, participated in it, and lived it. My reason for writing this is to share what I have learned and experienced with you and others in the family of God who are in need.

We see a tragedy on the evening news. A child has been killed in a senseless drive-by shooting. The parents, neighbors, friends and even the media reporters appear to be devastated. After the initial shock has faded, the survivors declare themselves barely able to continue on with life. Such circumstances are difficult to understand and even more difficult to reconcile and embrace.

A large tanker runs aground in the North Sea. The resultant huge oil spill threatens the area wildlife and the ecology of the surrounding coastal areas. Dire predictions are made by knowledgeable scientists and observers. Survival of some of the aquatic creatures and water bird population is a hope, but a gloomy outlook is prevalent.

A lead singer in a rock group in New York City is convicted as a drug user and dealer and sentenced to jail. Everything appears to be headed toward defeat and a life of crime, but something happens to interrupt the process. He meets Jesus Christ and the struggle for survival is changed to a life of victory. Today he is my friend. He has a home filled with love and victory and has a successful prison ministry. He now leads other condemned men out of their bondage and into victory.

In our present day society, being a victim has become a popular, almost acceptable, expression of one's life circumstances. Sad as it may be, this acceptance of mere survivalism has infected the Christian community. The young man who was jailed for drug dealing found his ultimate victory in Jesus Christ. Yet many Christians, who should be walking day by day in the victorious life of Christ, find that they are captive to the carnal world's concept that survival is the best they can hope to attain.

It makes me very sad when I hear a Christian respond to the question "How are you?" with "I think I am going to make it". This is why I felt the need to write this book. I want to hear a strong, positive, triumphant response that says, "Glory to God in the highest, I have great victory in the Lord Jesus Christ."

Many who are classified as victims of some injustice or ill-fated circumstance *do not even* survive. Many others *merely* survive. However, there are those, like my friend the rock singer, who move from their circumstances to become *more than* survivors; they become winners.

Here let us deal with five areas of our lives that encompass many smaller sub-areas. First we will consider emotions, as this area is essentially internal and precedes the others which are more outward in their context. Later we will examine relationships, finances, and communications. These three areas face us daily, and always involve others around us. The last area for consideration is faith, which is an ultimate that is our final point of victory over the world and all it's problems. We have included some actual examples of people with problems in the areas we discuss to help make our discussion more personally relevant. All the names used are, of coarse, fictitious.

I have tried to set forth adequate scriptural guidelines so that the hungry, hurting believer can find a principle, directly from the Word, to help him in his very real place of need. Down through the years I have seen peace come to troubled and distraught men and women. I have seen emotions healed and joy come into lives and hearts. I have seen husbands and wives reunited, children and parents reconciled, and brothers and sisters brought into righteous relationships. I have seen financial battles won and Mammon pushed from his throne. I have seen barriers that thwarted good communications fall before those who learn to communicate Christ. I have seen faith rise to defeat the subtle lies of the enemy, and that same faith break forth into ministries which bring edification to others in the body of Christ.

My prayer is that everyone who has a need will read this with faith and an obedient heart, and that every such reader will move into the victory that the Lord Jesus purchased for all of us.

"How priceless is your unfailing love! Both high and low among men find refuge in the shadow of your wings. They feast on the abundance of your house; you give them drink from your river of delights. For with you is the fountain of life; in your light we see light." (Psalm 36:7-9)

PART ONE—EMOTIONS

CHAPTER ONE

GOOD & BAD

*I*n a recent city council meeting in a small town in mid-America the conflict between the members grew to such proportions that the chairman proposed a motion that all of the members treat each other with courtesy and respect in order that the work at hand might be accomplished. The motion passed. Before that meeting concluded, however, one member had to be expelled from the meeting because of his profane and violent language aimed at the other members. He was the chairman, the man who had proposed the motion for courtesy among the members.

It may be amusing to consider how this man's emotions caused him to become the brunt of ridicule because of his inability to control them and his resultant actions. Yet all of us, at times, are victims of our own negative emotions. The emotions themselves are not necessarily the ultimate villains, but the way we handle or fail to handle these strong feelings often become villains. Improper handling of our feelings can contribute a strong adverse impact on our daily lives and undermine the quality of our Christian walk.

In our consideration of emotions, we must not fail to emphasize that there are both good and bad emotions. Bad, or destructive, human emotions could be classified as attributes of the flesh or even of Satan. Good, or edifying, emotions can then be recognized as attributes of God which are expressed through the processes of our thoughts or feelings.

Lest we consider all emotions as undesirable, let us point out that there are four good, godly emotions that merit consideration and definition. These are emotions in a broad sense, but emanate from attributes of God. What we acknowledge as good emotional "feelings" are in reality *His person* and *presence*. These are expressed by our responses to His attributes.

First we must acknowledge *love*. Love is, or should be, a strong emotional factor in each of us. God is love, and every Christian with a healthy spiritual life will freely confess that he loves God and that God loves him. We can build love by an act of our will and submission to God's will. The presence of that God-given love is the least self-serving and the most beautiful of all the emotions that we experience.

In the deepest sense, we acknowledge His presence by our actions which indicate His love in us. The natural man's comprehension confuses many carnal feelings with love: i.e. affection, sympathy, physical attraction, and even lust; but these are very inadequate substitutes for the godly love that results in our willingness to lay down our lives for one another.

Second, *compassion* is also a godly emotional attribute which should be cultivated and exercised. Our Lord Jesus had compassion on the people of Jerusalem because they did not recognize the time of their visitation. This was such a strong emotion that He wept over the city. When we experience compassion toward others in their place of need, we reflect the heart of the compassionate Christ.

In our fleshly feelings we may sometimes do seemingly compassionate deeds, but for reasons that are self-serving. True compassion from His heart is righteous and unassuming and does not seek a return on investment. He sees us at our worst, knows our failings and faults, and yet empathizes with us in our great need. His grace works in us when we experience true compassion toward others.

Third is *peace*. Peace appears to be a very passive emotion, yet it comes as a result of righteousness and is a highly desirable and much sought after emotional state. There is no true rest without peace. The world would sometimes define peace as the absence of war, but this is a very inadequate concept. Peace is a component of the expression of the Kingdom of God. It can be found in the midst of the battle or the storm, and delivers us from the anxieties of the world around us.

As in other good emotions, peace is ultimately an expression of God's person and is a gift of God. It is "not as the world gives", but is founded in Jesus Christ's promise to give His peace. It is rooted in righteousness, and without righteousness peace eludes us. When we enjoy His imputed righteousness and practice righteous ways, peace ensues.

Finally, *joy* emanates from peace, and joy is a most highly desirable emotion. Joy is deeper and more permanent than the emotion referred to as happiness and far beyond the shallow momentary experience the world calls "fun". Every man who attains to real joy in Jesus Christ can count himself richly blessed. He has tasted of God's Kingdom.

This joy that comes from Him is our strength. The Scriptures promise us that when we meet Him He will bid us to enter the joy of the

Lord. However, even with this promise for the future, godly joy is available to all who walk in His righteousness and obtain His peace.

These four good emotions are usually not in evidence when we are victims of bad, or ungodly, emotions. When fear, malice, hatred, sorrow, grief, bitterness, resentment, anger, jealousy, anxiety, etc. are predominant, or even residual in us, we find that love, compassion, peace, and joy are at best overshadowed, if not missing altogether. Under the yoke of these bad emotions, we are unable to draw on the delightful benefits that accompany the good emotions.

There is a tendency to adopt the attitude that outside influences are to blame for all of our bad emotions, and that we cannot really do anything about them nor rid ourselves of their hold.

This is a misconception and an unscriptural belief. Many of these tormenting emotions are the direct result of our own failure to face facts and to see things in the light of the love of God through Jesus Christ. Other negative emotions, although prompted by outside factors, remain as our thorns in the flesh simply because we do not seek to overcome them, and sometimes we may even embrace them unwittingly.

How can we extricate ourselves from the grip of the unrighteous and ungodly feelings which usurp our benefits in Christ? Let's see what the Scriptures say about the source of these victimizing emotions.

We can start with the fact that the Apostle Paul includes many of the emotions listed above as works of the flesh.

In Galatians 5:19-21 Paul wrote, " The acts of the sinful nature are obvious: sexual immorality, impurity and debauchery; idolatry and witchcraft; hatred, discord, jealousy, fits of rage, selfish ambition, dissensions, factions and envy; drunkenness, orgies, and the like. I warn you, as I did before, that those who live like this will not inherit the kingdom of God." (NIV)

The belief that we cannot do anything about these emotions is a lie from Satan. Jesus said that He whom the Son sets free is free indeed (John 8:36). He has the answer that takes us from that survival mode of carrying the extra baggage of bad emotions to the victorious mode of liberty in Christ.

One method which can move us from survival to victory is given us in I Peter 2:1-3. " Therefore, *rid yourselves* of all malice and all deceit, hypocrisy, envy, and slander of every kind. Like newborn babies, crave pure spiritual milk, so that by it you may grow up in your salvation, now that you have tasted that the Lord is good." (NIV)

Peter tells us to rid ourselves of these undesirable and unacceptable emotions and activities. The King James version says "lay aside". We obviously *can* lay aside the problem emotions; thus, winning over these elements becomes our responsibility.

Lest we view this as a mind over matter situation, or, worse yet, as a humanistic endeavor where man reigns by his positive self-will, we need to understand the interplay between man's will and God's will.

God's will cannot be thwarted, nor can it fail to be accomplished. Yet He has given into the realm of man's dominion a **free will** that permits a man to do and think as he chooses. This freedom of choice is a marvelous privilege. It is also a dangerous gift which must ultimately be subjugated to God's will to avoid self destruction.

The key to victory can be found in the same realm of choice that is so fraught with danger; our choice of whether to **lay down** our own will, or to **exercise** our own will instead of looking to God's will.

We must remember that our salvation came to us because Jesus Christ submitted His fleshly will to the will of the Father. When our Lord Jesus faced the cross for our salvation, He sought the strength for the right choice through prayer.

In Matthew 26:39 we read, "My Father, if it is possible, may this cup be taken from me. Yet not as I will, but as you will." And again in verse 42, "My Father, if it is not possible for this cup to be taken away unless I drink it, may your will be done."

Jesus' flesh was subject to strong emotions in this crisis. Death is the most feared and most avoided of all circumstances and events that we humans face in this fleeting life. Yet our Lord, by His willful act of choosing the Father's will rather than the will of the flesh, was able to submit His own will, die for our sins, and overcome the awesome specter of death. When He died to His own will, that death brought life for all of us who believe and also choose the Father's will for our lives.

King David likewise cried out in Psalm 40: 8, "I desire to do your will, O my God; your law is within my heart." Although he was sometimes driven by strong emotions, David was always able to come back to a place of submission to God and His will. He wrote his songs and fought his battles with fervency of spirit, but when confronted with the righteousness of God and the will of the Father, he was able to let the wisdom found in obedience bring him to the end of his own will and the acceptance of God's will.

In the next chapters let us examine how to overcome some of the more common destructive emotions that cause even devout Christians to live lives of survival rather than victory.

CHAPTER TWO

FEAR

*F*ear is a universal emotion. Very small children and very old people all share the emotion of fear. The word "phobia", which merely means fear, is applied as a suffix to many categories of our lives. For example claustrophobia is defined as an abnormal dread of being in closed or narrow spaces. Phobia usually indicates a strong or exaggerated fear of circumstances, an object, or a class of objects. The implication is always that fear is bad. Although this is generally true, we find that at least one category of fear can be good or beneficial.

We read in Proverbs 9:10 "The fear of the LORD is the beginning of wisdom: and the knowledge of the holy is understanding." And again David says "The LORD taketh pleasure in them that fear him, in those that hope in his mercy." (Psalm 147:11). The fear that God generates in the hearts of men is obviously righteous, commendable and beneficial. It always results in mercy from God. Lowly, created man was made to fear, love, and worship the great Creator who both made him and redeemed him. Here, however, we will address some *destructive* fears that man so often feels in his daily walk.

1st John 4:18 says "There is no fear in love; but perfect love casteth out fear: because fear hath torment. He that feareth is not made perfect in love." The fear that we experience apart from the fear of God is like an octopus. It spreads its tentacles in many directions. The singular word "fear" could generally be expressed in the plural as "fears". It sometimes seems like a position or vantage point from which we view multiple circumstances or possibilities as objects which portend of bad times ahead, or a repetition of unpleasantness which has transpired previously. Fear can influence our actions, our attitudes and our relationships. It is both destructive and debilitating.

Fear can originate from natural phenomenon, from imagination, from a demonic source, or from other sources or circumstances, but it can be conquered by our faith in God. When a demonic fear is exorcised, it can return again unless we have overcoming faith. Psalm 27: 1-3 says, "The LORD is my light and my salvation—whom shall I fear? The LORD is the stronghold of my life—of whom shall I be afraid? When evil men advance against me to devour my flesh, when my enemies and my foes attack me, they will stumble and fall. Though an army besiege me, my heart will not fear; though war break out against me, even then will I be confident." Many things appear to be the objects of our fears. David saw enemies, foes, armies, and war as the agents of the attacker, yet he saw his defense as stronger than all the enemy.

We, likewise, may have many agents which attempt to bring fears into our lives, but when our hope is in the Lord and we are confident in our relationship with Him we can overcome the fears and rout the enemy so that he never has dominion over us. When we fear poverty of the flesh or of the spirit, we can hear His voice saying "fear not, for I am with thee". And we remember Jesus' words in Luke 12:32, "Fear not, little flock; for it is your Father's good pleasure to give you the kingdom."

Alice—From Fear to Faith

A young lady, we will call Alice, was a victim of fear in many areas of her life. She feared for her relationships and for her own self worth. Every time she encountered anything that seemed in any way controversial, she required an affirmation of the love that others had for her. Anger and damaged relationships were by-products of her fears and lack of self worth, and she needed emotional support and counselling on a weekly, and sometimes daily, basis.

Finally, after many sessions and frequent prayer, she began to come into a place of faith. She began to believe the counsel she was receiving, such as that we are covering in this book, and to declare Scriptures of faith. She had an emotional turnaround. Victory came and she began to laugh and enjoy a victorious Christian life. Today Alice is a happily married woman, a great delight and a strength to her husband, and a friend to those that she formerly feared. The anger is gone, and her relationships have been restored.

We can overcome fear every time we believe the promises that God has made to us in the Scriptures, and when we proclaim faith by speaking these promises aloud in the face of the fears that try to attack us. We must not just *think* faith, but *speak* it. Jesus spoke aloud to the wind and the sea when the storm arose on the lake. Again He cried out in a loud voice when He called to Lazarus to come forth from the tomb. We should literally speak the word of faith to overcome if we want to be truly victorious over fear. We can appropriate a word of faith from the Scriptures to declare aloud to attain our victory. You *can* overcome *every* fear by the Word that you appropriate from the Scriptures.

Jesus Christ, the living Word, is *your* victory. Declare it and proclaim it, and you can move past survival to victory.

CHAPTER THREE

ANGER

*E*ven little babies, who cannot talk or understand conversation, feel and express anger. Much of the violence that erupts as civil unrest springs from anger. No one can say honestly that he has never experienced this emotion. In Galatians 4:20 this "act of sinful nature" is variously called "wrath" (KJV), "fits of rage" (NIV), and "outbursts of anger" (NAS). These are very descriptive expressions of something we witness in people's actions frequently, if not daily.

Anger finds its roots in our sensitivities. We all tend to want to defend our position, our possessions, our sense of being violated in some way, or any wrongs that we either see or imagine. Frustrations and inadequacies in any of these defensive areas result in anger, and anger is always an unreasonable emotion and one that frequently breeds violence.

When a Christian yields to anger and expresses it openly, he will always later feel remorse and he generally will repent at some point to get rid of the condemnation that follows an expression of anger. When anger is not expressed, it can smolder for days, weeks, months, or years.

Released anger can bring a wide variety of results. Sometimes it is only an embarrassment as was the case of our illustration of the city council chairman who had to be expelled from his own meeting. At other times it manifests itself through crimes of violence against others or even self-inflicted injury.

The Apostle Paul admonishes us "In your anger do not sin: Do not let the sun go down while you are still angry, and do not give the devil a foothold." (Eph. 4:26-27, NIV). Here we find several implications that deserve our attention.

First, Paul recognized that anger would come. He said "in your anger", not *if* you are angry. Because of our human frailties and our sensitivities we all tend to become angry at some point in time, and even

God's anger is mentioned many times in Scripture. Jeremiah 36:7 declares, "Perhaps they will bring their petition before the LORD, and each will turn from his wicked ways, for the anger and wrath pronounced against this people by the LORD are great." (NIV)

Second, we note that anger can be speedily overcome. We are commanded to get past our anger before the day ends. Expressed anger will sometimes tend to dissipate as time passes, but we cannot depend on this. However, we have the power and the authority to get past the season of anger quickly through the Word of the Lord in the Scriptures and the Word which He has placed in our hearts by the Holy Spirit.

We hear Paul's words *"do not let* the sun go down while you are still angry"*. The victory is ours if we can believe it. We can rule anger by speaking faith, by reliance on the Holy Spirit, and by exercising forgiveness toward whatever person or circumstance we believe to be at fault. We must look past our sensitivities to the facts of righteous behavior which we are taught by the Word.

Third, we find that this area of rule is necessary to avoid giving the devil a foothold in our lives or in the relational circumstances that are involved. Anger opens a door that permits Satan to exercise his strength unless we close it quickly. We must remember that he does walk about "as a roaring lion—seeking whom he may devour".

It is wise to keep this battlefield in the realm of overcoming the flesh and its weaknesses, rather than permitting Satan to choose the times and places of conflict. He would love to bring in his demonic spiritual influences and bind God's people over to his subjection and his encroachment into their lives. But, if he has already gained a dwelling place strong enough to cause anger to be uncontrollable, remember that there is still deliverance available for all. If we rule anger by the Word of God in our daily lives, however, we can be victorious without ever opening the door for Satan's dominion.

Albert—Anger Burned Within

Let's talk about Albert's anger. He was a young man who had experienced a degree of successful ministry in the past, but who now found himself in a place where his ministry was no longer acceptable to the spiritual leadership of the congregation where he worshipped. He felt that he was limited to a very narrow expression of his giftings and callings in the things of the Kingdom of God. Anger resulted. It was deep seated and smoldering, and sometimes his attitude seemed to be only an expression of hurt, humiliation, and rejection, but a real anger burned within him.

Albert was a man who knew the Scriptures and, when he became able to apply them, the Holy Spirit was able to bring a real deliverance to him and in turn to his family. His faith enabled him to move into a new dimension of ministry, expand into new relationships, and revitalize some former relationships. Today he walks in a place of genuine victory with his ministry restored. This required some changes in many areas of his life, but Albert has come through from his survival mode to victory and fulfillment in his ministry and his daily life. His faith and faithfulness, and the realignment of his relationships has resulted in a fulfilling life with the anger and rejection far behind him.

Jesus counseled us to "Have salt in yourselves, and have peace one with another." (Mark 9:50 KJV) This is the salt of our covenant with Christ. This is the salt that has not and will not lose its flavor. This is the salt that exemplifies the presence of Christ and His prevailing Word in peace and in victory over every antagonistic emotion. Even in times of peace we must rule our spirit and claim the victory over anger through daily praise and worship. Especially claim it when anger attempts to come into your heart and rob you of victory.

In Ephesians 4:31-32 Paul counsels us to "Let all bitterness, and wrath, and anger, and clamor, and evil speaking, be put away from you, with all malice: And be ye kind one to another, tenderhearted, forgiving one another, even as God for Christ's sake hath forgiven you."

God has given us the power to "put away" anger, along with other wrong expressions of our emotions, and to replace these elements with kindness, tenderness, and a forgiving heart toward others. You *can* move from survival to victory in the realm of anger.

CHAPTER FOUR

RESENTMENT

*R*esentment is a primary pool of emotional evil that serves as a source, or launching pad for many other debilitating emotions.

It can be born out of jealousy, real or imagined failures, comparisons between people, or bitterness from the past. I have heard it described as a prison. Indeed it can bind people on a long-term basis, and condemn them to a life cut off from the joys of the presence of the Lord and from the fellowship that we should enjoy with His people and all His creation.

The by-products of resentment are too many to list in their entirety, but a few of them should be mentioned since they occur frequently and are emotional barriers within themselves. A list should include malice, hatred, corrupt communications, vain imaginations, dissensions, factions, envy, and a reclusive manner that tends to prevent fellowship with friends, family, and the body of Christ as a whole.

Like anger, resentment can either be hidden or overt. Many times we tend to hide our resentment just as we have hidden the jealousy, bitterness, etc. that generated it. Hiding our problems usually means even hiding them from ourselves. We lapse into denial. We put our heads in the sand. We actually invent lies, and "tell" them to ourselves and to others around us.

We must be honest with this insidious emotion and acknowledge its presence. Only then can we purge ourselves of this feeling.

When expressed overtly, this emotion is capable of causing conflict with others and generating the by-products mentioned above in all parties concerned. Expressions of our resentment typically manifest either anger or fears or both. It is easy to see how this emotion can and does isolate and debilitate those who fall victim to it.

The answer to being rid of this problem can be found in what Paul calls the "renewing of the mind". In Ephesians 4:22-24 we read "...put off your old self, which is being corrupted by its deceitful desires; to be made new in the attitude of your minds; and to put on the new self, created to be like God in true righteousness and holiness." (NIV).

To renew our minds we must not only put off the old self, but also put on the new self. When we put off resentment, we must replace that emotion with a new emotion. When we recognize resentment as unwelcome in our inner man, we must welcome in godly attitudes and emotions "in true righteousness and holiness".

Beverly—From Resentment to Blessing

Beverly's problems were born out of jealousy, an unhappy childhood, and an inadequate income and lack of fulfillment in her own home. She would never express the envy and resentment that she felt, yet in areas where she felt unfulfilled she would frequently resort to crying and times of depression.

Beverly's victory came when she found a place to center her love — in her child. Once she found a place to show love, she found that she could more readily receive love. She began to love those whom she had seen as enemies, and found that she could bless those that she had previously resented because they had material possessions and advantages she did not have. In the renewing of her mind, resentment fled and she found the grace to forgive others and to enjoy the victory that came from loving those whom Christ loves.

Resentment against another person must be turned into love and a right relationship. Prayer is the real key to accomplishing this. When we pray blessings on the target of our resentment, it changes something within us. Jesus said in Luke 6:27-28 "But I tell you who hear me: Love your enemies, do good to those who hate you, bless those who curse you, pray for those who mistreat you" (NIV). As we pray and bless we will find that God brings a peace to our hearts no matter what occurs in the hearts of others. The resentment will melt away as we take the position that Jesus takes of blessing even our adversaries. When we consider the grace that we have received and take on the mind of Christ, we will discover that resentment has been washed from our spirits.

You **can** move from survival to victory in this emotion through obedience to Christ's command, and you can also overcome all the associated destructive emotions, such as malice, hatred, envy, etc., in the process.

CHAPTER FIVE

THE KEY

*T*he whole of our society appears to be living on emotions, and it relies on rationales to make those emotions apply to daily life, relationships, morality, and even understanding God and eternity. Of course in many people today there is avowed agnosticism, and some even profess atheism. This too frequently comes from unrighteous emotions and feelings along with fears of the future, and an inability to face the reality of dealing with righteousness and admitting that no one can actually manage his own life without God. Even in their defeated state, people need a hero, and so they turn to movies, sports and sometimes even witchcraft and the occult in order to find something beyond the reality of their own mundane, defeated, circumstances. This is a survival scenario, not a place of victory.

The body of Christ seems to be captured by the "feelings syndrome" in much the same way that unbelievers are captured. People use their emotions as a measure of their position in Christ and a measure of their ability to do the will of God. These feelings are very real, but in most cases they are not based on the Word that God has given, and they are diametrically opposed to the Scriptures. The inward search with the carnal mind is both futile and endless. It is a grasping for self-fulfillment that can never bring the desired results. Vain imaginations and accusations of blame toward others yield the fruit of sadness, sorrow, and loss of faith in God. Eventually we are faced with loss of confidence in the effectiveness of His Spirit working in us.

Husband and wife, children and parents, pastors and congregations all suffer divisions because of unscriptural feelings and emotions that are permitted to dominate thoughts, actions, and attitudes. The tragedy of our feelings-oriented society is that the Word of God is no longer the motivating force in our daily lives, our prayer lives or our efforts to extend the Kingdom of God.

However, we can correct this and turn our lives, our nation, and our witness into a victorious, vital, growing extension of the great and glorious Christ whom we serve! When love of God, love of righteousness, and love of one another are full, real emotions, there is no room for destructive and debilitating emotions. According to 1 John 4:16 "... God is love. Whoever lives in love lives in God, and God in him." (NIV) This shows us the place where complete deliverance from every bad emotion is available to all.

Charles & Christine—Overcoming Emotions

Although they had been married for many years, Charles and Christine were both victims of troubled emotions. Feelings dominated Christine so much that resentment and anxiety plagued her and brought a sadness to her spirit that negated any potential for joy in her life. Charles, although a soundly rational thinker and an intelligent, educated leader in his profession, was subject to the defeats, frustrations, and bitterness that emotional turmoil can impose. It sometimes looked as if the individual defeats they experienced would also result in the end of the marriage.

The advantage that Charles had was faith. He was a student of the Word of God and he refused to permit Satan to kill his faith. The ultimate turnaround was striking for this couple. Through prayer and persistence Charles was able to come to victory, and Christine was able to draw from his victory to find her own victory. Because they desired to overcome and were able to apply prayer, love and faith, they now are living in a place of victory that once appeared to be unattainable.

In the presence of the God of love we can find glorious victory over emotions from Satan, the flesh, and the world. In His presence there is fullness of joy. In Psalm 16:11 David declares, "You have made known to me the path of life; you will fill me with joy in your presence, with eternal pleasures at your right hand." (NIV) How deeply we need to dwell in this "presence". How desirable is the place near to Him, where nothing can overcome or defeat us. In 1 Chronicles 16:27 we read, "Glory and honor are in his presence; strength and gladness are in his place." (KJV).

The Lord Jesus has the door open for you to enter His presence, and there you find the victory. In John 6:37 we read, "...him that cometh to me I will in no wise cast out." This is personal assurance that you have access to Him whenever you need Him.

We should enter the door to His presence every day. Every time we realize that we are not conscious of Him and His nearness we should find time to enter that place where He is real and standing close to us. This is not a difficult thing, but as simple as the act of giving thanks, offering praise, and moving beyond ourselves to worshipping Him in spirit and in truth.

The Scriptures frequently remind us to lift our voices in thanksgiving and praise. Merely saying "thank you Jesus" in sincerity permits us to see the first small opening for our entrance through the gates and into the courts of the King. His will is that we move close to Him and live in that holy place.

Summary of Part One

Genesis 1:3 tells us, "And God said, 'Let there be light,' and there was light." Wherever His light shines the darkness must flee. Just as certainly as He gives us the light, He is the one who moves us from a survival mode to a victory mode in our emotions. Emotional victory is as complex as each individual's personality, but there are a few basic things we need to put into practice to attain victory in all our emotions.

A. **We must desire to be victorious over the unrighteousness of our bad emotions.** This desire must be based on our honest assessment of our problem areas which must be overcome.

B. **We must pray and believe that God hears and answers our prayers** for victory. In James' epistle we read that we do not have because we do not ask. Jesus Christ has given us clear promises that He will answer those prayers which we pray in His name.

C. **We must love God and our neighbors** with the same love that He has given to us. As we overcome unrighteous emotions, we must replace them with the righteous emotion of God's love.

D. **We must trust in the Word of God** more than our own feelings. The arm of flesh will always ultimately fail, but His Word will always triumph.

E. **We must speak a word of faith** which overcomes Satan and our flesh and takes us into His presence in accordance with His Word. Even our salvation results from the confession of our mouth according to Romans 10:10.

When we dwell daily in His presence, we can move out of a survival mode to a place of victory in our emotions through obedience to the Word of God, through speaking faith, through the love of God, and through overcoming the fleshly emotions as we let the mind of Christ dwell in us and rule in our lives. We can do more than survive, we can thrive. Let us trust in what God says, not on what our emotions tell us, and His victory is ours.

PART TWO— RELATIONSHIPS

CHAPTER SIX

THE IMPORTANCE

*A*fter examining emotions as our initial area of concern, the natural second area to examine is that of relationships. The natural man tends to base his relationships on his emotions. When we have conquered our emotional problems, we find it easier to comprehend and experience relationships as extensions of God's will and character. What is God trying to express to us about relationships? Let us look at this area with open hearts and minds.

God is a God of relationships. Father, Son and Holy Spirit are one. The covenants that He has made with men have been reliable, immutable and everlasting. The New Covenant in the blood of Jesus is our assurance that our salvation cannot be discounted by some subsequent circumstances that may arise in future times. God is a God of irrevocable commitments in relationships.

In Isaiah 62:5 the Word declares, "As a young man marries a maiden, so will your sons marry you; as a bridegroom rejoices over his bride, so will your God rejoice over you."

This verse paints a vivid picture of God's attitude toward relationships both in heavenly places and in earthly arenas.

Victorious relationships and joyous warmth and camaraderie are available to us as we walk the Christian path, yet we sometimes fail to even be aware of the value of our relationships and whether they are functioning or in distress. Mere survival is generally all that many people expect from life and their relationships.

Most of us would concur that marriage should be the most joyous of our human relationships, and that the Father is pleased with this righteous relationship. But we should also recognize that all relationships under Christ's caring love should be fulfilling and joyous.

Because many men have become insensitive to righteousness, they frequently suffer the deterioration of their best relationships without

Beyond Survival to Victory

ever even monitoring the state of those relationships. Yet, these same men will give great attention to natural functions of the environment around them. They attempt to understand the creation without ever knowing the ways of the Creator.

The scientific community is very careful to observe and monitor the condition of our physical habitat. The Pacific rim receives its fair share of attention, because of its volatile condition. The movement of the plates of the earth's crust and the volcanic potential is of grave concern to those who observe it and to the people who are potential victims of the effects it produces.

There are many known faults in the earth's surface, and these become the subject of much study and concern. Scientists have developed various measuring devices and techniques to monitor the movements and conditions of faults, as they become indicators of things to come in the regions they threaten.

The most notable and publicized fault here in the United States is the San Andreas Fault. This prominent and widely known fault in California has caused widespread damage from time to time, and there are predictions that additional and greater movement and subsequent damage lies ahead.

Three categories of devices that are used to measure the movement and potential movement along this fault are strainmeters, creepmeters, and laser electronic instruments. A strainmeter records the expansion and contraction of rock. A creepmeter consists of a wire strung across a fault and a measuring device. A laser electronic instrument records every quiver along the fault. Scientists utilize the data furnished by these instruments to predict future movements of the earth's surface. Thus with adequate warning the loss of life and property can be minimized.

Men are very concerned about these changes of the plates of the earth's crust. Earthquakes result. Proof of the results of these movements and earthquakes is in evidence in the orange grove trees that have realigned at the line of the fault, rivers that have changed courses, and destruction and deaths that have occured in many places. Everyone is interested in the damages caused by earthquakes.

Relationships are a lot like the plates of the earth. Relationships also are constantly changing, growing, drawing apart, coming together, suffering and yielding destruction, but few take the trouble to even measure how well or how badly their own relationships are surviving. It is time we took as close a view of our relationships as scientists do at the movement of the earth.

Looking again at the words of Isaiah 62:5, "As a young man marries a maiden, so will your sons marry you; as a bridegroom rejoices over his bride, so will your God rejoice over you", we find it very reminiscent of one of the apostle Paul's most familiar writings. Ephesians 5:28-31 reads, "In this same way, husbands ought to love their wives as their own bodies. He who loves his wife loves himself. After all, no one ever hated his own body, but he feeds and cares for it, just as Christ does the church— for we are members of his body. 'For this reason a man will leave his father and mother and be united to his wife, and the two will become one flesh.'"

Let us examine some of the relationships where we should have victory rather than just survival.

As Christians we should have a victorious relationship with the Lord Jesus. He has said that He would never leave us or forsake us. We in turn should certainly enjoy this most blessed position with the One who embodies all our hopes for victory now and hope of life throughout eternity.

We certainly can deduce from Paul's letter to the Ephesians that the marriage relationship is very much like the relationship between Christ and the church. Therefore our walk together with our husband or wife is of the highest priority, surpassed only by our walk with Christ.

Families and their individual and collective interactions are also very important, and constitute a whole arena of joy or sorrow, depending on how we relate. God is concerned for and interested in our family functions. Heritage and the extension of the future through our children are at stake, as well as the expansion of the Kingdom of God, as families reflect the Father's loving care for those who are His.

In the Church we have the potential for great joy and strength in our Christian walk as we relate properly with our brothers and sisters in Christ. Here we manifest God's family to the world by loving one another. We show that we are His disciples when we show that love.

There are many other less obvious categories where good relationships can be very beneficial and where bad relationships can be disastrous. Most people merely survive in their business and social interaction with others. Some though find real satisfaction and victory as they touch others, even strangers, and find that there are ways to relate properly to everyone.

The most amazing thing seems to be that most of us don't really know where we stand in many of our relationships. We see marriages suddenly fall apart and end in divorce. We see children become the losers as adults fail to maintain right relationships. We see families involved in vicious conflict over inheritances, over petty jealousies, over personality abrasions, and over old bitter disputes from the past.

We see churches divided, conflicts flare up between workers and employers, neighbors who won't speak, and business associates who despise each other.

Most of these "survival" or even "defeat" situations could have been resolved and victorious results could have been realized if the "earthquake" could have been foreseen. Why were there no warnings that the problems were real and imminent? We need measuring devices which will help us to determine the status of our relationships just as the physical scientists need devices to predict the movement of the earth's plates and the resultant earthquakes and volcanic eruptions.

CHAPTER SEVEN

MEASUREMENTS

*H*ow can we measure our status so that we can preserve the precious relationships that God has given each of us? God has His own standards and there are many signs that tell us how well or how inadequately we relate to Him and to those around us.

There are three plumb lines for the Kingdom of God given to us in Romans 14:17-19 "For the kingdom of God is not meat and drink; but righteousness, and peace, and joy in the Holy Ghost. For he that in these things serveth Christ is acceptable to God, and approved of men. Let us therefore follow after the things which make for peace, and things wherewith one may edify another."

Notice that righteousness, peace, and joy are "in the Holy Ghost". These are spiritual elements, and they can not be rightly understood by men with unregenerate minds. The Holy Spirit teaches us in spiritual realms so that we know and understand many things experientially in areas that are not comprehensible to those without Christ.

Observe also that, although the Kingdom of God is their source by the working of the Holy Spirit, these three work and produce fruit in relationships. When we possess them we are acceptable to God and approved of men thus finding victory in both the vertical and horizontal realms. The vertical realm represents the relationships between God and men, and the horizontal realm represents the relationships between men and other men.

To measure where we stand relationally we can use our scriptural "strainmeters", "creepmeters", and "laser/electronic" devices: righteousness, peace and joy,

Don & Doris—Missing Measurements

We can see in Don and Doris an illustration of a failure to measure their marriage relationships and the subsequent damage they suffered.

Don was unhappy with Doris, her attitudes, her appearance, and her activities, but he did not realize that his marriage was in trouble. Doris was also very unhappy with Don. She found him to be self-centered and oblivious to her needs. She saw him as a person to avoid and found more happiness in the times when they were apart than when they were together. Yet, even with all this evidence, she did not realize the precarious situation that their marriage was experiencing.

It took some heavy conflict and the intervention of a caring pastor before they recognized their deep troubles. When they "measured" their situation, they both realized that they could lose something very important to them. Because they loved each other and loved Christ, they were willing to change. Today Don and Doris have a warm, loving, stable marriage with Jesus at the center of their home.

You can't fix a car if you don't know what's wrong with it. The doctor can't prescribe medicine if he doesn't know what disease he must treat. In like manner, we must understand the relational problem before we can begin the process of healing, strengthening and bringing health to the relationship.

The world looks for these three measuring devices in the inverse order to the scriptural order. People seek joy, later they look for peace, and, as they come to the end of themselves, some look for or try to achieve righteousness. Let us look at these three in the order that God lists them, which is the order of their growth and fulfillment in us.

As we measure we will frequently use marriage as our most basic relationship example, because all of us are directly affected by some marriage or lack of a marriage. This may be primarily our own marriage, but can be our parents' or others from whom we have drawn our perceptions of relationships both good and bad.

CHAPTER EIGHT

RIGHTEOUSNESS

*W*e must look for some specific problems as we analyze and diagnose the status of our relationships. Let us ask some questions and answer them truthfully with a sincere desire to understand our own responsibilities in the procedure of moving from survival to victory in relationships.

Let us ask some questions concerning righteousness.

First, *are we selfish or selfless toward the other person or persons?*

Paul admonishes in Romans 12:10 "Be devoted to one another in brotherly love. Honor one another above yourselves". (NIV) Like all the scriptural principles, we find that this attitude is diametrically opposed to our society's attitudes. Each man seeks to promote himself. Everyone is devoted to his own agenda.

John's Gospel gives us even more stringent guidelines. In John 15:13-15 Jesus says, "Greater love has no one than this, that he lay down his life for his friends. You are my friends if you do what I command. I no longer call you servants, because a servant does not know his master's business. Instead, I have called you friends, for everything that I learned from my Father I have made known to you."

Laying down our lives, being friends with the Lord Jesus, and hearing and knowing the same things that Jesus learned from the Father is an inconceivable, yet true, expression of the right relationships that the Lord made available to us.

We must consider others first in brotherly love, honor, friendship, openness, and commitment to lay down our lives. Selfishness can never be a part of a righteous relationship, but selflessness opens every avenue for a flow of love toward others.

We should examine ourselves before we look for selflessness in others. We can not permit our judgment of others to dim our perception of our own attitudes. This key, which opens the door for righteousness, is vital for all who would have successful relationships in every area of their lives.

The Apostle Paul sums it up well in Romans 12:10 when he writes, "Be kindly affectioned one to another with brotherly love; in honour preferring one another". (KJV) This preferring simply means to be selfless by putting others ahead of ourselves.

It is all right to look for this attribute of selflessness in others, but *first* we should look for it in ourselves.

The second vital element we must look for is love! *Do we find love? Love is the pure essence of righteousness—God is love!*

In today's society love has many connotations. Trite feelings are sometimes deigned to be love by most of us. We love certain foods. We love the weather. Lust is frequently confused with love, as is romantic attraction between two people. But the godly love that Paul defines is pure and reaches far beyond the human emotions.

In I Corinthians 13:3-8 Paul declares, "If I give all I possess to the poor and surrender my body to the flames, but have not love, I gain nothing. Love is patient, love is kind. It does not envy, it does not boast, it is not proud. It is not rude, it is not self-seeking, it is not easily angered, it keeps no record of wrongs. Love does not delight in evil but rejoices with the truth. It always protects, always trusts, always hopes, always perseveres. Love never fails. But where there are prophecies, they will cease; where there are tongues, they will be stilled; where there is knowledge, it will pass away."

I Corinthians 13 is probably the most practical definition of the functional expressions of love ever compiled. We can make application of these plumb lines to our own activities, and "meter" whether we manifest these attributes. The repeated "always" aspects go beyond the ability of the natural man to fulfill them, but they do give us goals to pursue.

By the grace of God and the workings of the Holy Spirit we actually can attain to the high standards that Paul sets forth. Let us utilize this measuring device to see whether we are in reality walking in God's righteousness and in love.

The third question we must ask to measure our status is *Do we manifest real righteousness—practiced, not merely talked about or understood.* The old adage "actions speak louder than words", while not Scripture, is certainly a wise observation in the arena where we must practice righteousness.

Are we speaking without acting, or do we practice what we preach? I John 3:7 declares, "Dear children, do not let anyone lead you astray. He who does what is right is righteous, just as he is righteous."

How do we "do" what is righteous? We just do it! I saw a bumper sticker the other day that read, "Abortion! In your heart you know it's wrong". We are faced with many options, but we know how to choose and do what is righteous. Use this meter. Do we make the godly choice? Do we do what we know deep down inside is the right thing to do? We have the option to truly practice doing right in every situation. Sometimes it may be costly, but it is always worth the price.

We must judge ourselves, and measure the standard of our actions with what the Holy Spirit directs and what the Word of God declares.

We find another encouraging word in I John 3:10-11. "This is how we know who the children of God are and who the children of the devil are: *Anyone who does not do what is right is not a child of God;* nor is anyone who does not love his brother. This is the message you heard from the beginning: We should love one another."

With these principals to guide us, we can see where we stand in our righteousness toward others to whom we relate. But righteousness leads us on to another "meter", that of peace.

CHAPTER NINE

PEACE

*P*eace emanates from righteousness, yet we must find it and "measure" for it to see whether it is there, what is missing, and what circumstances prevent the fulness of peace within each person.

In Psalm 85:8-13 the writer declares, "I will listen to what God the LORD will say; he promises peace to his people, his saints—but let them not return to folly. Surely his salvation is near those who fear him, that his glory may dwell in our land. *Love and faithfulness meet together; righteousness and peace kiss each other.* Faithfulness springs forth from the earth, and righteousness looks down from heaven. The LORD will indeed give what is good, and our land will yield its harvest. Righteousness goes before him and prepares the way for his steps." (NIV)

We have the promise of peace to God's people in this psalm, but we find that, like most of God's promises, it is tied to some other aspects of God and His character. Love and faithfulness are obviously interactive and presumably interdependent. Love is certainly always faithful, and faithfulness which springs forth from the earth meets with God's own righteousness as it looks down from heaven. In verse 10 we find that love and faithfulness are components of righteousness, and righteousness aligns with (kisses) peace.

The one, two, three order in Romans, that of righteousness, peace and joy, are the elements of the Kingdom of God flowing down to man in God's own order. When we measure our peace we find it evidenced through or attested to by love and faithfulness, and it always has its basis in righteousness.

When we attempt to use our plumb line of peace and we find anxiety, frustrations, worries, fears, etc. it indicates that we have failed to achieve peace. Close scrutiny will reveal that underneath there is some sort of unrighteousness in the relationship.

In marriage there is genuine peace in the hearts of both the husband

and the wife when each is loving and righteous toward the other. In a family the peace is unbroken when love, trust, and security are abundant and each has a righteous heart toward the others. In a church, when every heart is like minded and the people walk together in a unity of the spirit and a bond of peace, we can find a place of rest and peace before the Lord Jesus.

When we measure for peace, what do we find in our relationships? Do we find that it is a delight to be with those who share our commitments and purposes? Or do we find those "little foxes" of differences that create pockets of criticism and resentment and bring schisms into the relationships and leave us with only survival instead of victory.

Peace is not just the satisfaction of getting our own way, nor the gratification of defeating our enemies. The peace we test for is rest in the Lord Jesus having His way, and the gratification of finding reconciliation and love with those who were formerly our enemies, but whom we can now love as friends.

Jesus said in John 14:27, "Peace I leave with you, my peace I give unto you: not as the world giveth, give I unto you...."Without the Lord Jesus the world around us can never know peace as we can know it. The world can accept a truce as peace. This is only a survival mode, not a place of victory. The struggles and trials can vanish from our hearts in the midst of the storms and the battles. This is victory in peace, not as the world gives, and this is what we are hoping to find as we meter our level of peace.

Wars come out of man's greed and striving for power, wealth, and personal gratification. Peace often seems to be only the absence of war. Yet, even the man of war desires to possess peace for himself and those he cares for. An Adolph Hitler or a Saddam Hussein would be pleased to have all his enemies defeated and crushed, with no one who could attack or threaten his domain. But God's peace which we seek is a simple peace based on the investment of all authority in heaven and earth in the God man Jesus Christ.

What we surrender in righteousness comes back to us through the hand of God to fill our every need and cause every relationship to be full, rich, and filled with the victorious presence of Jesus. In looking to find that peace which becomes our victory we find a simplicity that stretches beyond man's comprehension.

Zechariah 3:10 gives us a picture of that simple peace. The prophet declares, "'In that day each of you will invite his neighbor to sit under his vine and fig tree,' declares the LORD Almighty." "That day" to which the prophet refers is the day in which all sin has been removed from the land and righteous rule has been established. Remember that we must look for the simplicity of His peace when we test for peace in our relationships. Let us not permit our human expectations to blind our eyes because of its simplicity.

Even the elements of nature are beneficial only when they are at peace. The warmth of the sun and the soft, soaking rain makes the crops grow and mature for the harvest. The wildly blowing torrential rains that accompany a hurricane destroy the crops that the patient farmer has planted and tended, and he never receives the benefits of his labors from the harvest.

Isaiah 32:17 says, "The fruit of righteousness will be peace; the effect of righteousness will be quietness and confidence forever." Are we bearing the fruit of righteousness that brings peace into our relationships? Are we extending loving, peaceful care to those God has given us? Are we experiencing peace? We can know victory in God's peace, and go forward to the next area of victory, that of joy.

CHAPTER TEN

JOY

*J*oy is a goal for everyone, the ungodly and the godly alike. Men seek after it in their play and wise men even in their work. We all know when it is present and when it is absent. Men sometimes confuse fun or happiness with joy, but neither of these constitute that element which has an eternal composition. In Isaiah 51:11 we learn that "The ransomed of the LORD will return. They will enter Zion with singing; everlasting joy will crown their heads. Gladness and joy will overtake them, and sorrow and sighing will flee away".

Children have fun at birthday parties. Workers are happy when they get a raise or a promotion. These things are not the same as joy. Joy overtakes righteous men who walk in peace, and it is everlasting; durable for eternity.

Righteousness brings peace, and peace produces joy, but the Word, when it is received by hungry hearts, is the vehicle that opens the door for joy. There is an interesting and relevant passage in Nehemiah that illustrates the hunger that brings joy and the strengthening effects of received joy. This word came at the time that the wall around Jerusalem was completed and the nation of Israel was being restored to righteousness before God.

Nehemiah 8:8-12, "They read from the Book of the Law of God, making it clear and giving the meaning so that the people could understand what was being read. Then Nehemiah the governor, Ezra the priest and scribe, and the Levites who were instructing the people said to them all, 'This day is sacred to the LORD your God. Do not mourn or weep.' For all the people had been weeping as they listened to the words of the Law. Nehemiah said, 'Go and enjoy choice food and sweet drinks, and send some to those who have nothing prepared. This day is sacred to our Lord. *Do not grieve, for the joy of the LORD is your strength.*' The Levites calmed all the people, saying, 'Be still, for this is a sacred day. Do not grieve.' Then all the people went away to eat and drink, to send portions of food and to celebrate with great joy, because they now understood the words that had been made known to them.".

As we test our relationships for joy we find that grief, heaviness, sadness, weeping are all indicators that our joy is missing. When it is missing we are also missing the strength that we should have in Christ.

The Lord Jesus speaking in John 15:10-13 says, "If you obey my commands, you will remain in my love, just as I have obeyed my Father's commands and remain in his love. *I have told you this so that my joy may be in you and that your joy may be complete.* My command is this: Love each other as I have loved you. Greater love has no one than this, that he lay down his life for his friends".

The joy that follows peace comes with God's blessing upon its presence. Jesus greatly desired that His followers should be filled with complete joy. That joy for Him was manifested by love, sacrifice, and obedience. That joy for His followers, while an inherited benefit, came through the same love, sacrifice and obedience. The joy was found in the midst of interactive, personal relationships.

All of our relationships should produce joy. Joy will be evidenced if the relationships are righteous and bring peace. When we are righteous, we receive peace, and joy springs up like a fountain, yet with the depth of an ever flowing artesian well which flows into a placid, clear lake.

Do we find this joy in our relationship with the Lord Jesus? Is it in evidence in our marriages? Does it give us strength in the family, the church, and other interactive relationships? This is why we need these meters: to test for the fullness of His righteousness, peace, and joy in our lives. No one else can fully apply the tests for you. You must examine yourself in integrity and honesty in order to move from survival to victory in your relationships.

CHAPTER ELEVEN

PERSONAL
APPLICATIONS

*H*ere we must apply the tests to some specifics in our lives. Look at your relationships and find the areas that are about to produce an earthquake. It is time to do something about our personal San Andreas Fault(s).

Man can do nothing but wait for the earthquake in California, but God has it in His hand. Yet God has given us the keys to His Kingdom so that we are not victims in our own circumstances. We do not have to merely survive in our daily fears and substandard relationships. He wants us to have victory.

He did not give marriages so that we might just endure, but that they might be sources of our joy in His Kingdom. He gives us brothers and sisters, relatives, co-workers, and friends in order that we might enjoy fulfilling relationship in the whole spectrum of our lives.

Edward & Emily—Restored Relationships

The marriage between Edward and Emily had a very bumpy start. Emily's father strongly objected to the union because of religious differences, and he would have literally stopped the ceremony if he could have. Over the years there remained a wall of division, until the young couple began to apply some of the principles presented here. They began to reach out in love, and to overlook the anger and hostility they received in return. They counted the cost and paid the price to bring reconciliation.

Ultimately they reaped the benefit of restored relationships. Today grandparents, parents, and grandchildren enjoy warm, loving times together because the principles of Christ were pursued and applied. Edward and Emily will leave a heritage of generations of love for their children.

To determine whether we want victory or only survival, let's ask ourselves three questions using the broken car as our analogy.

First, do we want the car fixed, or are we content to just have it sit in the garage or driveway? It won't start most of the time, and when it does we never know how long it will run before it stalls and leaves us stranded. It is dangerous to drive because it may quit in the middle of an intersection with eighteen wheelers bearing down on us. But do we want it fixed?

Next, we must decide whether we are willing to hear the truth about the extent and the expense of the repairs. Are we too limited and locked in to our own ways to be able to hear the truth? We know we won't like to hear what the cost will be, but are we open to hear the truth?

Finally, after we hear the cost estimate, are we willing to pay the price to fix it? There will be an economic sacrifice, but we will end up with a reliable, safe automobile. We can enjoy a happy outing with our family. We can even meet our appointments on time for business and social occasions. If we are willing to pay we will be grateful in the long run, and even enjoy the car that was such a problem in the past.

Fixing a marriage or any other relationship may require the above three steps to move from survival to victory. We must be open to face the facts. We must realize that God would have all our relationships to be life giving and joyous.

Embracing the process of change does require our commitment to both hear the cost and to be willing to pay. It is never easy to say "I was wrong." It is difficult to obey the Scriptures and to follow the instructions of the Lord, the righteous judge.

The best part of our obedience is that there is real victory when we are willing to follow His instructions. There is joy beyond our fondest hopes when we are truly rightly related to others and walking in the full confidence of our place in Jesus Christ. Let us look at the process.

After applying the tests for righteousness, peace, and joy in our varying situations let us consider the results of those tests. This becomes very personal. All of us must be honest with our own thoughts, conditions, and assessments.

What of our marriages? Is there love flowing in the joy of this God-ordained union? Do we find peace in each other's presence? Is the righteousness of open and full communication and sharing of one another's burdens bringing more and more oneness into our union daily?

How about family victory? Are our children ours or the world's? Do we find gaps in the warmth and loving care that we once knew? Is there the sweet order that comes from Christ's headship in the activities in the Home?

We can ask these and many other questions in every category of our relationships. We can use the perspective that we gain to help those around us to also find a new fullness and a victorious life in Christ.

If we have made realistic assessments and determined that we **want to have victory**, we are **willing to hear** the cost, and we are **willing to pay** the price, we can prepare for victorious times ahead.

CHAPTER TWELVE

HOW TO WIN THE VICTORY

W hat is our formula for implementing what we have discussed? How do we win a clear and lasting victory in the area of relationships? The starting place is in Jesus Christ. More definitively it is in His attitude and by His Spirit. We must be willing to embrace His attitude rather than clinging to our own old paradigms. We must hear His words as counsel and instruction for changing our ways, and then obey that counsel and instruction.

Frank & Faye—Sacrifice Brings Victory

Frank and Faye's situation illustrates the necessity of sacrifice to redeem some marriages. Both Frank and Faye had been married before, and came into the new relationship with some old habits and spiritual baggage. Things went well in the new marriage for a season, then the personal attitudinal differences began to emerge. Both Frank and Faye had habits and attitudes that they treasured and were reluctant to lay aside for the good of the marriage. They saw the problems, but did not understand how to measure for righteousness. They understood that the joy was gone, but did not realize that the peace that was required to bring joy was a missing element.

Professional counselling failed, and the situation was pronounced hopeless by the counselors who offered only divorce as a solution, but God's grace prevailed. It was Faye who was finally able to bring a degree of righteousness to bear on the situation. Faye's faith enabled her to lay aside her personal preferences and some of her former religious prejudices which were not necessarily scriptural. She now tried to please her husband rather than herself. Application of the principals we share in this chapter has made room for the Holy Spirit to redeem the marriage. Faye counted the cost, paid the price, and is now reaping the harvest of a happy home. Frank has also learned to exercise a degree of righteousness, but the victory was won by Faye's willingness to obey the Scriptures and live in the knowledge that God is indeed our ever present help in every situation.

In Luke 6:27-28 we find some very difficult and, as far as the world is concerned, seemingly irrational words. Jesus said, "But I tell you who hear me: Love your enemies, do good to those who hate you, bless those who curse you, pray for those who mistreat you."

This is not the way of the secular, business world, and sadly enough, not often of the church world. Men strive to inflict harm on their enemies. They hate back, and they curse back. If they pray at all, there is a predisposition to pray for harm to come to those who mistreat them. The "get even" syndrome predominates in our society and in most of the societies of the world.

Let's remember though that these people who walk in their own way are the same people who function in a survival mode at best. To find God's better way, what must we do?

We must see others as Jesus sees them. Only then can we see clearly. Only then can we empathize and offer grace to our detractors. Our attitudes basically come from things we have learned from others who did not see others as Jesus sees them. We have a new and living perspective that can cause us to see the man or woman that Jesus gave His life to redeem. We must see wives, husbands, children, parents, friends, business associates, and even brothers and sisters in Christ as He sees them. They were worth His provision of salvation. They are worth our love, our blessings and our prayers.

We must bless those that He blesses. This is basic but we resist doing it. Jesus said it, so it is not a suggestion but a commandment. When we look with our judgmental eye we find it easy to say "they don't look as though God has ever blessed them". But He has. In some it is obvious because of some outward sign that we can observe, such as money, health, or popularity. In others it may not be visible, but God has opened a door of salvation for even those who seem to be desolate and abandoned. This is a far greater blessing than great wealth or fame. Jesus loves all of them, and He loves you too.

We must realize that our marriages are sacred and covenantal, not contractual. When we look at our marriages as the world see them, we frequently fail to see them from God's perspective. Covenant before God is not like a contract of the world which can generally be broken and disregarded as circumstances change. Lack of covenant yields discord, distrust, and disintegration. Recognition and respect for covenant yields respect, love, trust and integration.

Each of us must learn to honor the other before himself. Only then can we find that victory that God gives to those who love and obey Him.

We must learn to eliminate the "yeah, but" response which prevents our becoming obedient to Luke 6:27-28. We all tend to rationalize away the very substance of our victory because it does not agree with our human comprehension and our worldly, fleshly mental concepts. **We must recognize that our concepts are not like God's concepts.** In Luke 6:32-33 we read, "If you love those who love you, what credit is that to you? Even 'sinners' love those who love them. And if you do good to those who are good to you, what credit is that to you? Even 'sinners' do that." This perspective that God has is always going to be at variance with our human perspective. The prophet Isaiah stated it very clearly when he said that His ways are not our ways and His thoughts are not our thoughts.

We must seek His presence as we come to accept His perspective in order to let that perspective become a part of us; not just something that we acknowledge as right. Then we can begin to apply His love and attitudes in our day by day relationships and experience greater victory then we have ever known.

We must learn to stand in the place of grace, not condemnation. This is a vital door to victory. In Luke 6:36-37 Jesus said, "Be merciful, just as your Father is merciful. Do not judge, and you will not be judged. Do not condemn, and you will not be condemned. Forgive, and you will be forgiven." What an amazingly simple option God has offered to us. To think that by the act of forgiveness we receive forgiveness. By avoiding judging others we can avoid being judged ourselves. If we can truly show mercy we will be like the Father. He is ever merciful to us. We are called by His grace, and we need His grace on all that we do. If we stand in our works we will be judged, but we can not permit ourselves to judge others or we will place ourselves in the courts of judgment.

We must recognize that all things belong to Christ and act accordingly. Our ability to properly perceive the world and all of creation is an indispensable element in achieving and maintaining victory on a continuing basis. We tend to use the possessive pronouns my, mine, your, and our as if we really were proprietors rather than stewards of the people, things, and circumstances with which we deal day by day. King David cried out in Psalm 24:1, "The earth is the LORD'S, and everything in it, the world, and all who live in it;'. Even the people that we relate to are the Lord's. We must be aware of this truth and apply it in specific, practical ways to those with whom we walk and relate.

Summary of Part Two

Let's look at a list to help put this in a practical context that may trigger additional awareness of how we relate. For brevity we will look primarily at the husband and wife relationship.

A. **See our wife or husband as a child of the Lord,** not as our servant or our antagonist. He or she is a precious gift that we steward for Christ.

B. **Consider our own will or desires as secondary** to the one we love and live with. Be considerate and conscious of the ways in which we make demands or enforce our own desires on our beloved.

C. **Look for ways to bless and bring joy to our spouse.** If we will be sensitive to the needs and desires of one another, each trying to please the other, we will both reap great rewards.

D. **Forgive and forget all of the past problems** we may have had. Remember that love keeps no records of wrongs. Just as God has a sea of forgetfulness, we must erase the past affronts and discord and walk in a spirit of peace.

E. **Set our affection on our own beloved.** Express our love verbally. Show it by our actions. All of us need the overt expressions from our loved ones that reassure us that we are loved.

F. **Find time to read the Scriptures together.** Read aloud to one another and listen to the encouragement, wisdom, comfort, and faith that the Word brings.

G. **Pray together,** in agreement and in submission to each other's will. Let the Lord Jesus bear our burdens, heal our wounds, and solve our problems as we cast all our cares upon Him.

H. **Love one another** and be willing to lay down our lives for each other as Christ has done for the church and for each of us.

This is the Apostle Paul's counsel in Ephesians 5:23-33, "For the husband is the head of the wife as Christ is the head of the church, his body, of which he is the Savior. Now as the church submits to Christ, so also wives should submit to their husbands in everything. Husbands, love your wives, just as Christ loved the church and gave himself up for her to make her holy, cleansing her by the washing with water through the Word, and to present her to himself as a radiant church, without stain or wrinkle or any other blemish, but holy and blameless. In this same way, husbands ought to love their wives as their own bodies. He who loves his wife loves himself. After all, no one ever hated his own body, but he feeds and cares for it, just as Christ does the church—for we are members of his body. 'For this reason a man will leave his father and mother and be united to his wife, and the two will become one flesh.' This is a profound mystery—but I am talking about Christ and the church. However, each one of you also must love his wife as he loves himself, and the wife must respect her husband."

Let us hear carefully all that Paul spoke and obey the Word for our marriages. We should apply parallel principals to all our other relationships. As we walk in the presence of the Lord Jesus, we can test ourselves for righteousness, peace, and joy in all our relationships. If we apply these principles that can cause us to thrive, not just survive, we can walk in His victory.

PART THREE—FINANCES

CHAPTER THIRTEEN

WHO'S IN CHARGE?

*H*aving looked at our emotions and our relationships, we must consider an area that is vital in all of our daily lives, but which is often ignored as an "unspiritual" area. It is amazing how many of our relationships are based on financial concerns, and how much financial things influence our emotions. Here we must permit our understanding to go beyond checkbooks, bills, savings accounts, and numbers. We must view this as an arena where we gain our victory by the Spirit of the Lord.

In the Gospels the Lord Jesus mentions one great challenger against God. This is of course the great, demanding "god", Mammon. In Matthew 6:24 we read, "No one can serve two masters. Either he will hate the one and love the other, or he will be devoted to the one and despise the other. You cannot serve both God and Money."

Mammon is really a stronger word than money. Mammon means wealth, or avarice, making it in a sense, deified. Mammon becomes a "god" to those who worship it, consciously or unconsciously.

If we rule our finances, they won't rule us. If we regard our wealth as important it will become an idol. The rich young ruler came to Jesus with all the law covered, but Jesus told him he lacked one thing; sell all, give to the poor and then follow Him. (Luke 18:22) If we see money and possessions as commodities that God has provided for us to share, he can trust us with more. Then we will not be subject to it, but will delight in ruling it so that we can share it.

George—Found the Secret to Giving

George is a godly man and a man of God. He has endured periods of economic privation at some earlier points in his life, but over the past few years he has fully realized who really is in charge. He recognized a few years ago that God had consistently met his needs. He was diligent in doing all things well and was very generous in supporting the needs of others, but he felt that he needed to establish a consistency in his financial commitment that would enable him to sow bountifully into the work of the Lord Jesus.

George set a standard for his financial needs, and committed to Christ that all funds he received in excess of those requirements would be given to help other people or ministries in their needs. Within a few months he received a check that would have been a year's salary only a few years before. He gave the entire amount to others who were in need. A short time later he received another check for ten times the amount of the first check. It was enough to pay off the mortgage on his home with some left over, but he took none of it. Without hesitation he divided the proceeds of the second check to several places where there were needs. George found the secret to receiving from God's fullness, and he continues to prosper. God will never let him down.

I have watched and listened many times when deliberations were made by sincere men to decide what paths to follow in areas of their own lives or in the lives of those for whom they were responsible. Many times the final solution was determined by the bottom line economic results. I have seen people come for prayer or counseling, ostensibly to find the will of God, yet too frequently the questions seemed to center around financial motives and sometimes involved the search for personal monetary gain.

When Satan wrestles us down so that we are grasping after economic gain for its own sake, we become subject to his persecution and ultimately to his humiliation. It is like a cat and mouse game. The cat has all the fun, and we become mice waiting to be tormented and then devoured.

Mammon is a hard taskmaster. God is a jealous God. If we insist on giving some of our loyalties and allegiance to an economic deity, it becomes idolatry, and we find ourselves under the hard taskmaster rather than the loving and benevolent God who redeemed us.

Let us look at five principles that will give God room to bless us financially without our becoming subject to the forces of financial pressures that would dominate us and ultimately destroy us.

The first and most obvious of these is that we must **labor diligently**, in whatever our hands find to do, always realizing that it is God who gives the increase.

Our mandate for this dates all the way back to God's pronouncement to Adam in Genesis 3:17-18. The ground was cursed because of Adams disobedience so that its fruitfulness became available to man only through toil. We only "eat bread" by the sweat of our face. The man who does labor diligently does prosper, both in provision for his daily needs and in spiritual things, if he labors in the Lord.

Paul substantiates this premise in Ephesians 4:28 when he says that a man should labor with his own hands, performing what is good so that he may not only have sufficient for himself, but he may also have something to share with others who have needs. He also goes so far as to say that if anyone will not work, neither shall he eat. The old Puritan work ethic is still a viable and effective principle for every Christian to follow.

We must not be reluctant to give ourselves to any honorable task. According to Proverbs 20:13 if we love sleep we will grow poor, but if we stay awake we will have food to spare. There is a similar admonition in Proverbs 10:4 where we are told that lazy hands make a man poor, but that diligent hands bring wealth. Diligent hands are obviously blessed.

I have observed people from other countries enter the American culture and find steady success. They are typically very happy to be in an environment where they have the liberty to work without fear, and they pour themselves into any type of work that they can find. Some have come from positions of prestige or high educational positions, and some from the most lowly backgrounds, but all seem to have a strong desire to give themselves to whatever labor is presented to them without complaint. The whole family seems to join together to produce and provide for one another, and they rise to a level of economic substance although great diligence is required of all of them. God's principles work even for the unbelievers.

The second principle which we must employ is that we must **rule our finances** well and never be slothful in "business". No matter how much money or substance is coming into our hands, we will still live in a place of survival rather than victory if money rules us.

Jesus gave us a clear example in Luke 14:28-30. This is the story of the man who started to build a tower. The man, who did not rule or have knowledge of his own financial condition, found himself subject to ridicule from all the observers because he had only a foundation with no superstructure, and then ran out of funds for the rest of the building. This was not a very good tower. It is no wonder that ridicule and finger pointing resulted.

When we try to accomplish anything that requires financial expertise, we should have all the facts. Then we should also have the wisdom and rulership over our own whims and indulgences that let us use the facts in a righteous, wise, constructive, and practical manner. We must know the needs and the sources of our supply to act in wisdom.

Ruling our finances is not the same thing as stinginess. Although in times of extreme need we may be required to exercise restraint in spending, we should never act out of motives which would cause us to unduly hold back monies because we either have a fear of loss or we have a love of money. Paul writes in I Timothy 6-10 that the love of money is a root of all sorts of evil, and that some by longing for it have even departed from their Christian faith and caused themselves great pain. If we resort to stinginess and think of that as ruling, we really are submitting to mammon as our idol and become as bad off as those who exercise all their efforts to get money.

We must be prudent, not stingy, not lax, nor a spendthrift, but we must handle financial areas with diligence and wisdom. Proverbs 21:28 teaches us that there are stores of the best of food and oil in the house of the wise, but that a foolish man eats all that he has. If we handle the increase that God gives in wisdom, the source will not dry up.

The simple mechanics of controlling our handling of what we do have is vital if we are to know victory in our economics. Budgets are very helpful tools for controlling our spending. Yet, it is perhaps even more important to have a budget, and then to compare our budget to our actual income and our spending. This will give us a greater understanding of where our available money goes.

It has been said that budgets are made to be broken. Another way to express this is to say that a budget is only a guideline, but must never become a taskmaster. Here we are not attempting to teach budgeting (there are many experts who do teach in this area) but we want to acknowledge that budgets are only tools to help us as we follow God's principles. He is our source, and we must always be aware of this fact and adhere to His principles.

In the area of ruling, or controlling, our finances, we must stress that we need hearts that are committed to ruling, yet free to hear what God may say to our hearts. Our natural, carnal minds tend to make decisions based on the input from the world around us, but God can lead us into righteous, scriptural ways of financial decision making.

Keeping accurate, clear records of our finances is representative of the attitude that we should maintain in our spending habits. If we don't know what we spend and where we spend it, we certainly cannot determine how to correct problems. Keep records and make good, godly financial decisions based on sound knowledge and assessments of needs, purposes, and goals.

The need for consistency in our approach to our personal financial affairs is evident. God is a God of order. The seasons are consistent from year to year; summer follows spring and winter follows autumn. The sun rises every morning.

We, in turn, must be consistent in adhering to all the principles that help us to rule. There is a tendency from time to time to cast off restraints and forget our careful planning. We must remember our goals and purposes. When we save on a regular basis, we accumulate equity. When we invest in the things of the Kingdom of God, we store up treasures in heaven. Monetary investment is most certainly not the only way we invest in spiritual areas, but it is one way that we can express our dedication to His Kingdom, and it is also a way to bless others in accordance with scriptural precepts.

These principles keep us in touch with our source, so that we may enjoy the abundance that He supplies.

Principle number three involves our commitment. We must **commit all that we have to God**. Men everywhere find it important to defend what they deem to be their own possessions, whether it be honor, relationships, power, or material wealth. Yet in the wisdom of the Holy Spirit, the Apostle Paul writes in I Corinthians 6:19-20 that we are not our own, but we have been purchased with a price. Hence even our bodies, souls and spirits really already belong to the One who redeemed us. He emphasizes this again in I Corinthians 7:23 by saying that we were bought with a price, the blood of our Lord Jesus, and that we should not become slaves of men.

As we study the Scriptures we repeatedly find counsel that we should not pursue the wealth of this world. Proverbs 23:4 declares, "Do not weary yourself to gain wealth, cease from your consideration of it". Certainly a lot of energy could be saved if we could fully grasp the fact that the earth is the Lord's and the fulness of the earth. He freely gives us all things. Why should we seek for things which will never be ours to keep, yet which we have in abundance because our gracious Father supplies all our needs from His abundance.

When we can truly acknowledge that what we have is not ours but His, we can care for the things that He gives us to steward with an open hand rather than a tightly clenched fist. How easy it becomes to surrender those things which we count as our own if we commit them to Him, and yet we will certainly lose those same things if we try to keep them. In II Timothy 1:12 Paul makes a strong statement of his persuasion that he is convinced that God is able to keep everything which he has committed unto Him.

When we acknowledge that all we have comes from Him, we see with a righteous perspective. Let us consider nothing as our own possessions, but all things as His. This attitude opens the heart of God to bless us in turn. We recognize that we are stewards and we are only stewards. Remember that a faithful steward enjoys the good things of the master's household.

A beautiful and practical position regarding what we think of as our possessions is given us in Proverbs 30:7-9, "Two things I ask of you, O LORD; do not refuse me before I die: Keep falsehood and lies far from me; give me neither poverty nor riches, but give me only my daily bread. Otherwise, I may have too much and disown you and say, 'Who is the LORD?' Or I may become poor and steal, and so dishonor the name of my God."

As we learn to commit all that we seem to have to Him, we will find a sweet victory over worries and fears. That victory removes us completely from a survival mode of self preservation.

There is a fourth elemental principle that we should all know and which should be taught to all children at an early age. It is to **share with others**. Even if we have been taught, most of us tend to forget or abandon that precept as we grow to maturity and we learn the self survival ways of the world around us. The same parents that teach their children to share toys, snacks, etc. with each other, will sometimes find themselves jealously guarding their own possessions. Children learn much from observation of actions; perhaps even more than they learn from instruction.

The "give me", "me first", and "that's mine" mentalities are encouraged and applauded in our society today. The principles of monetary gain and possessiveness tend to be ingrained into children as they grow, because faith, hope, and love have not been taught or respected as pertinent to current day lifestyles.

The "me first" generation has proven to be only a survival generation. Yet when our hearts are filled with Christian love, we find genuine victory in the principles of sharing and of honoring others before ourselves.

We can share in a real and practical way as God leads us. We must never withhold from God's people what God has given us to share. In Proverbs 21:13 we read, "If a man shuts his ears to the cry of the poor, he too will cry out and not be answered." This is reinforced by John's words in I John 3:17-18, "If anyone has material possessions and sees his brother in need but has no pity on him, how can the love of God be in him? Dear children, let us not love with words or tongue but with actions and in truth."

The sharing principle is actually a type of sowing. The principles of sowing and reaping are involved. As we give, or share, we find that we reap grace and prosperity. However when we abandon sharing in favor of selfish ways or attitudes, we find that we reap poverty. Poverty can also be described as an absence of prosperity, substance, or abundance. Poverty is mere survival, but abundance which comes from sharing, or sowing, is victory and brings great joy.

The prophet Isaiah teaches us a fifth principle which is to **abide in scriptural principles**. This will provide deliverance from greed if we learn it and practice it. Isaiah 58:6-7 tells us, "Is not this the kind of fasting I have chosen: to loose the chains of injustice and untie the cords of the yoke, to set the oppressed free and break every yoke? Is it not to share your food with the hungry and to provide the poor wanderer with shelter—when you see the naked, to clothe him, and not to turn away from your own flesh and blood?"

God desires to see each of us individually and the church corporately come into compliance with this expression from His own heart. There is deep, rich revelation in this passage from Isaiah, and it reflects the loving care that our Father has for everyone. Sharing does not require that we be wealthy, but that we share from whatever He has supplied to us. Sometimes when we see Christians struggling for economic survival, it may be because they have failed to obey this cry of compassion.

Here is the wisdom of the Kingdom of God which brings a deliverance from the yoke of financial oppression for both the man who gives and the man who receives. In Isaiah 58:10-11 the prophet emphasizes the blessings that follow the man who follows the Scripture, "and if you spend yourselves in behalf of the hungry and satisfy the needs of the oppressed, then your light will rise in the darkness, and your night will become like the noonday. The LORD will guide you always; he will satisfy your needs in a sun-scorched land and will strengthen your frame. You will be like a well-watered garden, like a spring whose waters never fail."

Paul instructed Timothy in I Timothy 6:17-18, "Command those who are rich in this present world not to be arrogant nor to put their hope in wealth, which is so uncertain, but to put their hope in God, who richly provides us with everything for our enjoyment. Command them to do good, to be rich in good deeds, and to be generous and willing to share."

Many of these scriptural principles have already been stated in the first four areas discussed, but we must all learn to comply with the Scriptures simply because they are His Word. Ultimately our own will must be broken so that it will conform to His Word. This conversion of our hearts will result in great victory.

Now we come to a big question. Who are we dealing with, and what does He want? We are dealing with a righteous God! He is looking for a people who will hear Him, love Him and do His will.

The prophet Haggai spoke for the Lord and defined the economic problems of his day. Haggai 1:6 reads, "You have planted much, but have harvested little. You eat, but never have enough. You drink, but never have your fill. You put on clothes, but are not warm. You earn wages, only to put them in a purse with holes in it."

The reason for the problems was simple, God's people were more concerned with their own welfare than with the will of God. God's concern was for the rebuilding of the temple in Jerusalem in that day, but we have an even greater commission. Our concern must be for the building of the spiritual temple of God. We are the living stones who are being built into a holy habitation of God by the Spirit. He is disappointed and displeased when we pour all of our finances, our energies, and our hearts into our own desires, our own "houses", and our selfish plans. Because of this unrighteous attitude, Haggai further declared in verse 9, "You expected much, but see, it turned out to be little. What you brought home, I blew away. Why?" declares the LORD Almighty. "Because of my house, which remains a ruin, while each of you is busy with his own house."

We are dealing with a righteous God who wants His "house", the Church, to be built for His habitation. We know who is in charge, and He wants to give us victory in our finances as in every other aspect of our lives.

CHAPTER FOURTEEN

THE SOURCE

*T*he next logical question is how do we find the source for victorious prosperity? Where is the source of our prosperity? What is it like to know His prosperity? It is not like our carnal minds would lead us to believe. It is unlike the arrogant, presumptuous ways of man's sources. God's ways are not our ways.

Jeremiah 17:5-8 expresses God's ways and His grace. "This is what the LORD says: 'Cursed is the one who trusts in man, who depends on flesh for his strength and whose heart turns away from the LORD. He will be like a bush in the wastelands; he will not see prosperity when it comes. He will dwell in the parched places of the desert, in a salt land where no one lives. But blessed is the man who trusts in the LORD, whose confidence is in him. He will be like a tree planted by the water that sends out its roots by the stream. It does not fear when heat comes; its leaves are always green. It has no worries in a year of drought and never fails to bear fruit'."

When the prophet declares that we cannot trust in man, it brings different connotations to different people. Most of us have been conditioned to consider that the knowledge of this world is the real truth. As we grow in Christ we can see more and more clearly that man's wisdom and plans are all very timorous and subject to revision. The wisdom of one generation becomes the foolishness, or "old wives tales" of the next generation. As the Apostle Paul tells us in II Timothy 3:7 they are "always learning but never able to acknowledge the truth."

Man is not our source. Man's ways are never adequate. We do however have an abundant source in the Lord Jesus. When we reach the end of man's resources, God's abundant supply has only begun. He is the creator, the way , the truth, the life, and is even the restorer of those things and times and seasons and years that have been lost. *We really can enjoy full provision in every season if we trust Him, and if we see the true riches.*

There will be no fear. We will have "green leaves", or constant life, and we will always bear spiritual fruit.

We must be conscious of the difference between faith and presumption as we seek to draw from the true source for our needs. Men who fail to recognize God as their source can overstep the bounds of God's will and plans through their presumption. God is a loving Father who desires the best for us in all things, yet His vision, plans, and purposes in us may not agree with our conception of what is best.

Harry—Found His Source

After years of diligent work and times of abundance mixed with times of financial struggles, Harry finally found that he had met a brick wall. Well meaning, but misled, advisors had helped to turn his economic situation into a disaster. Even his prayer life had suffered. He borrowed money every month to continue in his established life style.

Harry, however, had ears to hear and he found his source. He was able to accept sound spiritual and financial advice. The road to financial victory came more quickly than seemed possible. When he adopted solid, righteous principals, God met him. Today he is able to see victory in every aspect of his Christian walk, including his ability to sow financially into the church and the needs of others. Harry's income has also increased from prior seasons, and his life and home are now places of peace and prosperity as he sows himself into Christ.

It is vital that we approach the source of all blessings from the vantage point of the Son of God. When we come to our source with the mind of Christ, we will not be self-serving or presumptuous. In Philippians 2:5-8 Paul expresses this attitude very clearly, "Your attitude should be the same as that of Christ Jesus: Who, being in very nature God, did not consider equality with God something to be grasped, but made himself nothing, taking the very nature of a servant, being made in human likeness. And being found in appearance as a man, he humbled himself and became obedient to death— even death on a cross!"

How different is this Christ approach from that of the man who is busily seeking success with his own arm of flesh. There is a way that *seems* right to man but which ends in defeat and disaster. God can only trust the true riches to those who regard them as they really are: the property of the Creator. In like manner God gives genuine, long-term, economic success to those who recognize Him as the actual source of that success. God can only trust the true wealth to those who don't want it for themselves.

Many who seem to be very affluent in the world's wealth are in reality living a lie and are in violation of God's principles. They have gained what appear to be economic empires through methods that are in disagreement with the Word of God. We have seen some of these empires tumble in recent years, and seen the unrighteous ways of the "Emperors" bring them down from their thrones. Don't envy men who have amassed great "holdings", because these "holdings" may in reality be forerunners to curses, rather than evidence of God's blessings.

We must not choose the wrong source! This is made clear in Habakkuk 2:6-7, "'Woe to him who piles up stolen goods and makes himself wealthy by extortion! How long must this go on?' Will not your debtors suddenly arise? Will they not wake up and make you tremble? Then you will become their victim." The NAS version says that such a man "makes himself rich with loans". This is vividly illustrated by the acquisition of large corporations through "leveraged buy-outs" (i.e. junk bonds, etc.). The whole foundation of these empires is based on cloaked and usually deceptive financial representations.

God has a better way! Proverbs 21:21 says, "He who pursues righteousness and love finds life, prosperity and honor." This verse is a paradox and it can easily be misunderstood as we attempt to apply it. If we want life, prosperity, and honor, we must not pursue it, but must rather pursue righteousness and love. Everyone wants life: He is the source of life. Everyone would like to have prosperity: He is the source of our prosperity. Honor can only come from Him who has all honor and is worthy of all honor, Jesus Christ, King of Kings and Lord of Lords.

How do we receive these blessings? Only if we do not want them for ourselves. We must pursue righteousness and love. Jesus said in Matthew 6:33, "Seek first his kingdom and his righteousness, and all these things will be given to you as well." This paradox is God's way of setting us on a right path to enable us to handle prosperity. As our source, He is wise to entrust us with the exact amount that we can handle without it causing us to veer from the path of His righteousness and His love. When we seek Him for provision in times of need, He certainly is able to supply all our needs according to His riches in glory by Christ Jesus. He will freely give us all things as we look to His righteousness first, and do not become distracted by our desires for prosperity.

In I Corinthians 3:6-7 the Apostle Paul states, "I have planted, Apollos watered; but God gave the increase. So then neither is he that planteth any thing, neither he that watereth; but God that giveth the increase."(KJV) Paul was the most prolific of all the apostles, yet he recognized the source of the growth and increase in the church. Like Paul, we must never forget our source. Jobs, inheritances, and investments all can be channels through which God can bless us, but we know our source. Job possessed twice as much after he passed the test because, "After Job had prayed for his friends, the LORD made him prosperous again and gave him twice as much as he had before."

We must always remember that *God* is the one who *gives the increase*. He is our source, and we are the winners. The promises are valid and, when we choose Him and not Mammon, our victory is assured.

CHAPTER FIFTEEN

HEARTS NOT SMARTS

We must consider that this victory is a matter of our hearts and ways, not our abilities.

Jeremiah 17:9-11 tells us, "The heart is deceitful above all things and beyond cure. Who can understand it? 'I the LORD search the heart and examine the mind, to reward a man according to his conduct, according to what his deeds deserve.' Like a partridge that hatches eggs it did not lay is the man who gains riches by unjust means. When his life is half gone, they will desert him, and in the end he will prove to be a fool."

God is interested in our hearts' attitudes. He searches our hearts and examines our minds. He desires to reward us, but a good reward is contingent upon our hearts and attitudes. Our conduct and deeds reflect the condition of our hearts. Victories in monetary areas, or any other areas of our lives, are contingent upon the thoughts and intents of our hearts.

God will not permit us to gain riches by unjust means and enjoy the fruit forever. Such a man may hatch serpent's eggs in the sorrows, sickness, unrest, and unhappiness of his wealth. We must permit Him to give us hearts of love and righteousness, lest we prove to be fools in the end.

Economic victory is really premised on righteous hearts and minds. If we seek with our whole heart to give our lives to Him, the Lord Jesus provides an abundance of life for us. If we seek to preserve our own lives, or to gain for ourselves, we will lose what little we seem to have.

We would be derelict not to mention that God really does expect something of His own people. Obedience is better than sacrifice. Malachi 3:8-12 declares, "'Will a man rob God? Yet you rob me. 'But you ask, "How do we rob you?" 'In tithes and offerings. You are under a curse—the whole nation of you—because you are robbing me. Bring the whole tithe into the storehouse, that there may be food in my house. Test me in this,' says the LORD Almighty, 'and see if I will not throw open the floodgates of heaven and pour out so much blessing that you will not have room enough for it. I will prevent pests from devouring your crops, and the vines in your fields will not cast their fruit,' says the LORD Almighty. 'Then all the nations will call you blessed, for yours will be a delightful land,' says the LORD Almighty."

The man with a righteous mind and sincere heart will desire to obey the precepts of God. These verses are familiar to most Christians who have attended church services on even a semi-regular basis. However, they may have become trite to many of us because of much exposure to them. We must have a clear understanding of the reality of the blessings that are associated with the obedience required by this word. In any case, it is still a heart matter. "Giving to get" is an unrighteous attitude which leads only to survival. When we recognize the privilege of "getting to give", however, and rejoice in the giving, we become recipients of God's blessings and win the victory.

Irving—Faithful to His Heart's Direction

Ever since his conversion to Christ, Irving had been a man whose desire was to please God. However, after several years of marriage and hard work, it seemed to be all in vain. He found himself burdened with debt, far behind in his income taxes, and he was advised to declare bankruptcy. He had a large family and a strong dedication to their welfare, but his dedication to be righteous was primary in his heart. He had faith that God would let him care for his family and overcome the financial deficit. With the help of a wise and faithful God, Irving began his turnaround.

In his diligence Irving worked two and sometimes three jobs for a season. One of these was in his own fledgling business. He lived with economic moderation and wisdom, and he was faithful to hear wise professional counsel and to obey it. He recognized his true source of provision and was faithful to fulfill his own heart's direction to both tithe and give to others whenever possible. He lived by scriptural precepts in every department of his life. Today Irving is a successful man with a thriving business and several employees. His children are all successful and outstanding in their school efforts and their service toward God. His faithful wife runs a home filled with hospitality toward others. Irving is a useful servant and fruitful in bringing others to Christ. God's blessings are evident in all that he does.

There is a portion of Scripture that is a microcosm of the heart attitudes of all who obey and live righteously as citizens of the Kingdom of God. This is a summation that Jesus gave to all who can hear and it expresses His own heart and laid down life. It is worth while to look at this section of Scripture to have it fresh in our hearts, so that we may enjoy its privileges as we are confronted with its high callings.

Luke 6:27-38 reads, "But I tell you who hear me: Love your enemies, do good to those who hate you, bless those who curse you, pray for those who mistreat you. If someone strikes you on one cheek, turn to him the other also. If someone takes your cloak, do not stop him from taking your tunic. Give to everyone who asks you, and if anyone takes what belongs to you, do not demand it back. Do to others as you would have them do to you. If you love those who love you, what credit is that to you? Even 'sinners' love those who love them. And if you do good to those who are good to you, what credit is that to you? Even 'sinners' do that. And if you lend to those from whom you expect repayment, what credit is that to you? Even 'sinners' lend to 'sinners,' expecting to be repaid in full. But love your enemies, do good to them, and lend to them without expecting to get anything back. Then your reward will be great, and you will be sons of the Most High, because he is kind to the ungrateful and wicked. Be merciful, just as your Father is merciful. Do not judge, and you will not be judged. Do not condemn, and you will not be condemned. Forgive, and you will be forgiven. Give, and it will be given to you. A good measure, pressed down, shaken together and running over, will be poured into your lap. For with the measure you use, it will be measured to you."

The road to victory in every department of our lives is set out in these verses, and the fulness of financial victory is expressed in the last verse. To him who can hear and obey, the results are assured.

CHAPTER SIXTEEN

YOU WIN

I have a friend whose life is an illustration of the principles we have set out in the previous chapters on financial victory. He has an outreach which provides for the needs of many who are poor both economically and spiritually, and he trusts God to provide for these many needs. Although he is reliant on God's provision for him and the people he serves, when another outreach need comes to his attention, he is the first to give. He sows and God provides.

Over the years God has enabled him to provide food, clothing, love, and the Gospel. He is now sowing into the third generation of needy who come to him. He is ministering to the grandchildren of some who first came to him years ago as children. The local church which he pastors has a rich vibrant ministry of the Gospel. The outreach which God has given him to oversee has become a testimony, and has become a fulfillment of II Corinthians 9:8-10, "And God is able to make all grace abound to you, so that in all things at all times, having all that you need, you will abound in every good work. As it is written: 'He has scattered abroad his gifts to the poor; his righteousness endures forever.' Now he who supplies seed to the sower and bread for food will also supply and increase your store of seed and will enlarge the harvest of your righteousness."

This brother in Christ is a winner. He is victorious because he followed the righteousness presented in the Scriptures, both in word and in deed.

Remember that the most glorious fact in your life is that Jesus loves you. He wants you to win and have victory in finances as surely as we all have victory in our salvation. His desire is that we find that place in Christ where victory is assured and awaits us. We discover the place in our own hearts, in the laying down of the hindering aspects of our past mindsets and attitudes. Only through death can we know a resurrection. Resurrection is the ultimate victory.

In Psalm 112:1-3 we are encouraged by these words, "Praise the LORD. Blessed is the man who fears the LORD, who finds great delight in his commands. His children will be mighty in the land; the generation of the upright will be blessed. Wealth and riches are in his house, and his righteousness endures forever." The psalmist further tells us that it is well with the man who is gracious and lends, and that God has given freely to the poor.

God's great care for the poor and desolate is evidenced in many Scriptures. Jesus admonished His followers to sell their possessions and give to the poor. He exhorted them to provide purses for themselves that would not wear out, a treasure in heaven that would not be exhausted or stolen, and where moths could not destroy it. When we give we win, when we grasp for ourselves we lose.

There are four things that God has revealed that He is going to restore in the times in which we live. They are: one, first love, along with the zeal; two, compassion toward all in need; three, our testimony, which is only effective if given in love and compassion; and four, care for the poor and desolate. These are all vitally needed, but the care for the poor and desolate is the key to the prosperity of the churches and each of us individually. Read Isaiah 58: 6-9 and you will find that this passage confirms that this care and compassion represents God's heart.

Summary of Part III

The world around us does not see financial success in the same way that God sees it. To help us to apply this "different" approach to financial victory, we present the following list as a review of some of the principals presented in the text.

A. **Labor diligently.** We must appreciate the privilege that God has given to us to engage in fruitful works, and know that He can bless us in every category of our efforts.

B. **Rule well in financial areas.** We must not let our finances rule us. We must know the facts of our own income and expenses, and understand these areas in the light of God's attitudes toward wealth, generosity, and righteous consistency.

C. **Commit all that we have to God and His Kingdom.** Remember that it all comes from Him by His grace, and He will entrust an adequate supply as He freely gives us all things.

D. **Remember to share with others.** God's own nature is to give. Just as Christ gave His own life for us, we are told to lay down our lives for our brothers. We must never close our hearts to the cry of those in need.

E. **Always handle your finances in accordance with scriptural principles.** We can not make righteous decisions or handle our funds profitably without obedience to His Word. We must not put our hope in wealth, but in God who gives the increase.

F. **We must know our source.** God is our source. We understand this simple fact, but we must also know Him as our guide, our provider, our example, and our redeemer.

G. **We must have His heart.** His ways are not our ways, therefore we must pursue His heart and attitudes. Be doers of the principles of Luke 6:27-38.

If we can hear what the Spirit is saying to the churches in this day, there awaits financial victory along with all the other victories we seek. Where is our treasure? Our hearts will be where our treasure is stored. If God's victory is in our hearts, and Mammon has no place there, we do not have to settle for financial survival. We can be winners. We can have victory and enjoy the abundance of His Kingdom.

"Do not be afraid, little flock, for your Father has been pleased to give you the kingdom." (Luke 12:32)

PART FOUR—
COMMUNICATION

CHAPTER SEVENTEEN

LIFE OR DEATH

*A*nother vital part of our daily lives that we could easily ignore is the area of communications. Whether we are dealing with emotions, relationships, or finances we are always in the business of communicating. The substance and the expression of what and how we communicate can sometimes make or break any or all of the three areas already discussed.

Proverbs 18:21 reads, "The tongue has the power of life and death, and those who love it will eat its fruit." If what we communicate with our tongues can bring life or death, it is easy to believe that real victory comes out of good communications. It further stands to reason that poor communications will yield, at best, only survival. How we communicate and what we communicate present a very broad spectrum of possibilities.

All of us to some extent live by communicating. This is obvious in the case of a salesman, a politician, a teacher, etc., but not always so obvious, although just as true, for a housewife, an electrician, or a professional football linebacker. The quality of their communications skills frequently determines the extent of their ability to produce income or to get the desired results in their field of activity.

What we tend not to realize is that we frequently end up in a survival mode instead of a victory mode in our lives because of our communications. Now we are talking about more than just earning a living; we speak of the very essence of our daily lives and even our eternal destiny. We do in fact eat the fruit of the life or death that we speak with our lips.

It is, indeed, amazing when we realize that God has given us the power of His Word in our communications in order that we might speak life and victory to others, and for our own benefit. This word power is the same power that He spoke about in John 1:1, "In the beginning was the *Word*, and the Word was with God, and the Word was God." John unfolds the depth of this statement in the next verses. He, the Word, was with God in the beginning, and the creator God did make everything that exists by this Word which is God. This is difficult for mere men to comprehend. John further says that "without Him nothing was made that has been made."

This communication, which is the Word, is creative. Therefore, we must grasp the vital importance of our own communications day by day. His creative Word and His communicative Word are not different but are alike, and certainly the great communicator is our Father God. In Genesis 1:3 we read, "And *God said*, 'Let there be light,' and there was light." Light itself can become communication. It reveals truth and makes manifest everything around us. Visual communication is only possible because of light. All of nature is constantly speaking of the presence, the grace, and the life of this Word which became flesh and dwelt among us.

In nature we can frequently hear the sounds of God's creation echoing the voice of the creative Word. If we are aware of God's presence and His desire to speak to our hearts, we can hear Him in many circumstances and situations.

One morning I saw a little bird on our apartment balcony rail. The weather was cold and it was snowing. The bird was similar to what we refer to as an English Sparrow, probably a House Finch. It had some red markings: a red head, a red throat and some red on its wings placed so that it appeared to have a red spot on its back when its wings were folded. It was obviously a part of a larger flock that I had seen earlier on the same rail, but this one sat all alone in the below freezing temperature and began a most unlikely function. It began to sing. It was a chirpy, bright crisp song, and to me it seemed to say, "Laud and Honor, Glory and Praise to God who rules and reigns over all the earth. Thanksgiving and Worship and Adoration to the One who supplies all things to the little ones who rely upon Him and trust Him to give the daily sustenance for every need." He sang his song of joy and flew away, doubtless to partake of the breakfast fare that the loving Heavenly Father had abundantly supplied for his need, even on a cold and blustery winter day. That morning that little bird communicated God and His grace to me.

This incident gave me sharp recall of an event early one summer morning when I lived in Texas. I was leaving a hospital where I had been visiting a church member who had undergone surgery. As I walked across a large parking lot, a mocking bird sitting atop a tall light pole began to sing a beautiful melody. As I walked by, the bird flew all the way across the rather large area to another pole on the other side. The song never stopped. It sang in flight all the way across the lot, never breaking the intricate melodies as it flew. The melodious song seemed to say, "All is well; there is great joy this day". Again it was as if glory and praise were being rendered to the great Creator who gave the new day and supplied every need according to His riches in glory in Christ Jesus. This was a song that communicated victory, not just survival.

The Gospel was communicated, not hidden. Victory was spread abroad by songs through the little birds He made and cared for. God who commanded the light to shine out of darkness was shining forth to show the knowledge of the glory of God in Jesus Christ.

In sharp contrast to the victorious sounds of the birds, the defeated world of men around us seems to be filled with "information" which predicts or proclaims only survival or death. The info-media is continually communicating the problems and defeats of the day. Grim predictions concerning the economy, unemployment, national and world politics, etc. flood our newspapers, our televisions, and our radios. Sarcasm dominates the editorials, the investigative reports, and even the humor. Survival is presented as the best for which we can hope. The alarmist sounds of impending doom always predominate, and the good things that could be reported are usually overlooked. We hear it on every hand. Men's actions and attitudes reflect this attitude of the media with a survival mode as our only hope.

We who have met Jesus Christ should be filled with thanksgiving that we do not have to be held captive by this attitude of defeat which Satan's communications attempt to impose on us every day. We have not only a note of victory for ourselves, but also a message to declare to all those around us that there is victory in Jesus Christ. Our communications are founded in the Gospel of God's grace, and we must be faithful to fulfill our part in declaring the victory that He gives. How do we attain victory for ourselves and communicate life to others? Let us examine our communications and the potential for victory.

CHAPTER EIGHTEEN

WORDS & BEYOND

*A*lthough we communicate to others, and they to us, primarily by our words, there are really many ways we communicate. Let us examine some of the many ways we impart our thoughts, our emotions, and even what we are to one another.

Certainly the first level of communication we must acknowledge is our **speaking**. Almost all of us speak thousands of words every day, and many of these words are spoken with very little forethought. We often speak from our emotions, and thus communicate only our personal responses to our circumstances. At other times we rely on our rational conclusions and communicate only what the carnal mind can conclude is the most important thing of the moment. In special times we may truly find ourselves hearing, and consequently speaking a word of faith which embodies the victory that always comes when God speaks.

More often than we realize we also communicate by **gestures**. So-called "body language" frequently gives evidence of victory or bare survival in a person's life. A man can sometimes shake his fist and communicate more agitation and anger than his words can convey. A woman can manifest a seductive smile and communicate her feelings to a man very effectively. The smile and happy hand clapping of a child on Christmas morning can express a world of delight and happiness that is joyous to every one who sees it. A heart touched by the presence of the Holy Spirit may show tears and adoration, and uplifted hands can express praise and worship toward the Lord.

Our **actions** indicate and communicate what we are and where we are going. If we get into a car and start the engine, it becomes obvious that our intentions are to go somewhere. If we get out the lawn mower and start it, it is apparent that we intend to cut the grass. If a man works diligently on a physical job, we can surmise that he will accomplish something and that he is willing to extend himself for his own or his family's needs. If one gives freely and generously to his church, we easily recognize that he has a dedicated heart.

Our **attitudes**, while usually expressed verbally, can be shown by our choice of reading material or entertainment, by our tone of voice, or even by our failure to speak. Silence can reflect moods and temporary reactions, or can be an expression of aloofness because of preoccupation, concentration in deep thought, or even a prayerful attitude.

No matter how we communicate, we do communicate. Those around us are drawing conclusions from what we say and what we show by our actions. We must also realize that we eat the fruit of our communications. According to Proverbs 18:21, "If we sow life we reap life, if we sow death we reap death."

All of our interaction with others is a platform of communication. As Christians, our desire should be to sow life. Our tongues have a most obvious, powerful influence on others, but all that we communicate, by any method, is a part of our sowing. We desire to make a positive impression on others, but in order to do that we must rule our communications in every category of our lives. In James 3:13 we read, "Who is wise and understanding among you? Let him show it by his good life, by deeds done in the humility that comes from wisdom."

Jack–Shadow of Rejection

Well educated and competent in his profession, Jack was unhappy nevertheless. He felt or imagined strong rejection by others around him. Although he was loved by his friends, he carried the shadow of rejection from the past and it showed up in his attitude, his actions, and his speech. He tended to isolate himself and he refused to be comforted and integrated into the healthy, happy social life of others around him. But somehow God was able to penetrate the shell that evidenced only bare survival to those around him, and to bring him to a place of victory that spoke victory through him to others.

Without becoming arrogant or self-assertive, Jack became one who communicated faith and found the will to do what he heard God speaking to him. As he communicated faith to others, he became a man who showed the faithfulness of Christ in both word and deed. It took time and a willingness to change, but over the years God has given him a lovely wife and family, along with a testimony of what Jesus Christ can do when we both speak and do His will.

We can have victorious communication beyond our words if we show it by our good life. It is interesting that James said that humility comes from wisdom. As we grow in wisdom, we will find that arrogance and haughtiness have no place in what we manifest to others. Victorious communication is exemplified by showing the humble Spirit of the Lord Jesus to everyone.

Non-verbal communications which communicate our weaknesses lead to no more than survival. On the other hand, non-verbal communications which show righteousness can bring victory.

CHAPTER NINETEEN

SELF REVEALED

*T*he source of our communications begins within our hearts. We communicate either life or death based on the condition of our own inner man. There is a very relevant Scripture in Matthew which gives us insight into this fact.

In Matthew 12:33-37 we find the words of Jesus, "Make a tree good and its fruit will be good, or make a tree bad and its fruit will be bad, for a tree is recognized by its fruit. You brood of vipers, how can you who are evil say anything good? For out of the overflow of the heart the mouth speaks. The good man brings good things out of the good stored up in him, and the evil man brings evil things out of the evil stored up in him. But I tell you that men will have to give account on the day of judgment for every careless word they have spoken. For by your words you will be acquitted, and by your words you will be condemned."

This Scripture prompts us to examine our hearts. What is stored up there? We must make as honest an appraisal as we can if we are to move our lives and communications from only a survival mode into a victory mode. Let's see what we might have stored up that could block our victory.

Do we have **selfish desires and goals**? When we only consider our own likes, dislikes, purposes, possessions, and pursuits we isolate ourselves from God's will. Wrong motives are almost synonymous with selfishness. When our motives are wrong and based on self-serving goals, we forfeit victory in our communications. Our words will condemn us rather than acquit us.

Resentment and failure to forgive others also defeat us. Our hearts can never be clear and righteous when we are bound in the prison of resentment toward others and toward circumstances past or present. We must forgive. We must be washed of old resentments. We must learn to put God's ways and will before our own feelings-oriented lives.

Unconfessed sins and failure to repent keep us in a bondage and condemnation that can destroy our ability to enjoy the good things of the Kingdom of God. Unconfessed sin is always unforgiven sin, but "if we confess our sins He is faithful and just to forgive us of our sins, and to cleanse us from all unrighteousness."(I John 1:9 KJV) The results of our failure to repent and receive forgiveness can not only destroy our ability to communicate victory, but can also leave us with fears and weaknesses and even doubts as to our own worthiness or usefulness.

This is only a partial list, for Satan will always attempt to keep us in a place of defeat, and in a place where we speak death when we speak from the abundance of our hearts. When we find defeated hearts, we can be grateful that God's grace also provides a solution.

It would seem to be a staggering thing for us to overcome all our stored reserves of problems and hindrances to victory, but the solution is really simple if we truly desire to go from death to life in our communications. Let's look at the solutions to the problems mentioned above.

We can remove "self" from the number one position. By putting Christ first we can replace our selfish desires and goals with desires for that which is best for the Kingdom of God. Putting Him first also includes putting others ahead of ourselves.

Katherine & Ken—Putting Christ First

Katherine was raised in a Christian home and was a very bright young lady. But she was given to being defeated in her daily life. She truly communicated woe and sadness to her friends and family. It seemed that the fears and anxieties that she bore were born out of her criticism of everything around her. She judged and analyzed continually, and, as a result, made others sad and miserable. Through His great grace, God gave Katherine a fine husband, Ken, who loved her deeply, but he also sometimes fell victim to her negative communications.

Because they were both faithful to trust God, He somehow brought new vision to both Katherine and Ken. They saw themselves as they really were, and resolved to change. This new purpose brought hope and a new ability to put self aside and Christ first. As they embraced their vision for future service to the Kingdom of God, they began to truly communicate joy and faith to others. Today to speak with them is a great delight. The victory that they share with each other has become a source of victory to others as they communicate Jesus Christ.

We must examine our motives and catch a vision for the Kingdom of God. Center all your motives in the heart of Jesus Christ and His motives. Be a servant to all those who are a part of His Kingdom.

If we will forgive, we will be forgiven. This becomes an act of our own will to be righteous. If we recognize the grace of God in our lives and give thanks, we can enjoy a place of great peace and joy that will make us communicate a sound of victory to all those around us.

When we doubt our own worthiness and abilities we are correct, because we all fall short in both categories. But we don't live by our abilities or worth. We should be thankful that we have a righteous advocate in Jesus Christ. He is worthy and He has the ability to do all things for us and through us. We can put all our trust in Him for only He is worthy.

Because He is faithful and just to forgive us of our sins, we need only to repent, desire forgiveness, and confess our sins, and we will be forgiven. If we resist the lusts that are from Satan, he must flee from us. Do not be fearful because of these negatives that we have discussed, because we have His love. Perfect love casts out fear, and the only perfect love is the love of God that comes through Jesus Christ and His perfect sacrifice for all of us. Acknowledge that His strength is made perfect in our weakness, and that He gives us His strength and His love freely.

We must see ourselves revealed as we truly are in order that we may become the competent communicators of the gospel of Jesus Christ that He wants us to be. As we apply these solutions and our hearts become clear and clean we are in a position to overcome the survival syndrome and move into a place of victory through the declaration and communication of all He has said and done on our behalf.

CHAPTER TWENTY

SPEAKING LIFE

We can communicate life and victory. Jesus said in JOHN 6:63 " The Spirit gives life; the flesh counts for nothing. The words I have spoken to you are spirit and they are life." We must realize that every word we speak has spiritual impact. We do communicate from the abundance of our hearts and thus slay or resurrect our hearers and ourselves by both our words and our deeds.

In James's epistle we are taught many lessons about our speech and our tongues. James 3:2 reads, "We all stumble in many ways. If anyone is never at fault in what he says, he is a perfect man, able to keep his whole body in check." The complete ability to rule what we say can elevate us to a position of perfection according to this verse. This puts an emphasis on communication that goes beyond the normal conversational aspects. We must be very aware of our speech habits and our non-verbal communications as well as our ability to speak well and communicate Jesus Christ in special circumstances.

In verses 3 and 4 James indicates that horses obey because of the bits that are put into their mouths, and that boats can be steered by very small rudders at the wishes of the pilot. It appears from these verses that our tongues may direct us more than we direct our tongues. If our tongues do indeed rule us, it appears that when we speak without the ruling influence of the Holy Spirit, we speak death rather than life.

The tongue is also likened to a fire, a world of evil. It sets forest fires and in a short time burns up the trees that took many years to grow. How many times have lives been reduced to ashes in a few moments of rash speech born out of anger, frustration, or despair? In verse six of James 3 the writer declares that the origin of this fire, which corrupts the whole person, is hell. All kinds of created beings have been tamed by man, yet no man can tame the tongue. James calls it "a restless evil, full of deadly poison."

In the wisdom of the Holy Spirit, James cited the incongruity of the use of our tongues. James 3:9-10 reads, "With the tongue we praise our Lord and Father, and with it we curse men, who have been made in God's likeness. Out of the same mouth come praise and cursing. My brothers, this should not be."

When we acknowledge that "no man can tame the tongue" we see that no man can win this victory without God's intervention, but God will freely give us the victory. It is more a matter of what we are than the words that we speak, yet our victory is a declared and living testimony as we give ourselves and our tongues completely over to Christ. Then we can speak and communicate righteousness to others.

Lewis—Cynical Communication

Lewis was a man who had seen many defeats and been in a mere survival mode for years. It seemed that everything he handled turned against him in the long run. He was very opinionated about any and every subject, and left no room for others to have their own thoughts and opinions. His communication was almost always critical and sometimes almost belligerent. The more he communicated his own ways, the more cynical he became. But God is faithful.

Although Lewis had reviled and alienated many, God broke through his shell of egotism and his judgmental words. Prayer and study of the Scriptures finally brought victory to Lewis. He changed his speaking from death to life, and the more he declares the life of Christ, the more he is able to enjoy that life. Today he is speaking words of reconciliation and forgiveness. Today he is more than a survivor, he is a victor.

Jesus said His words were spirit and life. When we truly walk in the Spirit, we will also speak by the spirit and will produce life and victory in those who hear. Having hearing ears is a vital element in receiving that life, and when we speak by the Holy Spirit, life becomes available to the sensitive hearers.

We must understand that we can also speak by a wrong spirit and death will result. If we can embrace the fact that the flesh counts for nothing, it will help us to seek to be filled with the Spirit. This is not an occasional prayer or a limited commitment to try to do better. This is a walk with the Christ of the cross and the resurrection. This is communion with the Father who cares for us every moment of every day. This is being filled with the Holy Spirit who is sent to us to help us and to indwell us.

In spite of all the warnings that James gives us regarding the tongue, there can be victory in our communications to others as we walk in the Spirit. We can speak by the spirit as we share the good news of Jesus Christ. John the Revelator tells us that this testimony is by the spirit of prophecy. Revelation 19:11 says that "...the testimony of Jesus is the spirit of prophecy." If this testimony is always inherent in what we speak, we will speak an anointed word that will bring victory to the hearers and manifest the victory of the speaker.

CHAPTER TWENTY ONE

ELEMENTS
OF VICTORY

What are the elements that we communicate that lift us beyond survival to the place of victory? What must we share, speak, and manifest? Let us look at some of the components of victorious communications.

Whether we realize it or not, **we communicate what we are**. Paul wrote to his beloved church at Corinth and called them "a letter from Christ." In II Corinthians 3:2-3 he says, "You yourselves are our letter, written on our hearts, known and read by everybody. You show that you are a letter from Christ, the result of our ministry, written not with ink but with the Spirit of the living God, not on tablets of stone but on tablets of human hearts."

We do show what we are, and if we are the Lord's, everyone will know it. People "read" people. We all are concerned with what the people we associate with really are. This is of greater concern than what they do or what they look like. The old adage "actions speak louder than words" is often true. If we are to represent Christ in truth, we must become His in all our ways and in our hearts.

As we share the reality of our relationship with the Lord Jesus *we* **must communicate thanksgiving**. The joy that a sure knowledge of our salvation brings should never be hidden. There is joy in victory, and there is victory in joy.

The Apostle Paul expressed the principal very clearly in the fifth chapter of Ephesians, which was really a gentle commandment to the Church. In verses 19 and 20 he says, "Speak to one another with psalms, hymns and spiritual songs. Sing and make music in your heart to the Lord, always giving thanks to God the Father for everything, in the name of our Lord Jesus Christ."

It appears that this admonition went beyond the meetings of the church, although it certainly included the meetings. He says "always giving thanks." There is great victory for us as we express the joy of our salvation in our daily lives and activities. This expression of singing, speaking to one another with psalms, hymns and spiritual songs will always communicate victory. Remember that even the birds of the air sing their praises of that victory.

If we communicate only our "human feelings" we only survive and only minister survival, but when we share thanksgiving with joy we communicate victory.

Even in this self-serving world we can **communicate blessings** toward everyone. In Luke 6:28 Jesus admonishes us to "bless those who curse you, pray for those who mistreat you." In this same passage we are told to turn the other cheek, permit our coat and shirt to be taken, and to give to everyone who asks without demanding anything back. These actions, born of obedience, manifest and communicate the victory that we have in our Lord Jesus.

In Luke 6:31 Jesus gives us the central Scripture for behavior in the Kingdom of God when He says, "Do to others as you would have them do to you." This "golden rule" is a basic principal of victorious communications. In this lies the key to representing the victorious Christ. It is evident that we must not minister condemnation but rather the blessings of Christ, in order that we might communicate and receive victory.

We fulfill one of the great needs in the world today when we **communicate hope.** I Peter 1:3 tells us, "Praise be to the God and Father of our Lord Jesus Christ! In his great mercy he has given us new birth into a living hope through the resurrection of Jesus Christ from the dead". Hope is a living, vibrant, enduring part of the Christian's life. When we communicate it, we bring victory.

Remember that others need the hope which you communicate. We all need hope in many areas. Even your spouse and your own family need to know the hope that you can share. One of the saddest phrases that a man can pronounce is, "I have lost all hope", but when we bring hope, we bring victory.

By the Word of God we **communicate faith.** Paul wrote to his friend Philemon about the encouragement that Philemon's faith brought him. In verses 4 and 5 Paul says, "I always thank my God as I remember you in my prayers, because I hear about your faith in the Lord Jesus and your love for all the saints."

Paul's loving care for Philemon becomes more obvious when he declares in verse 6, "I pray that you may be active in sharing your faith, so that you will have a full understanding of every good thing we have in Christ." Not only did hearing of Philemon's faith encourage Paul, but Philemon's sharing of faith gave him understanding. Paul's prayer for Philemon can be a pattern for us that we should *always* speak faith in *all* things to one another and to *all* men. When we follow this example, we exercise victorious communication, which truly communicates life.

How vital it is that we **communicate love** to those who do not deserve it. Jesus loved us when we did not deserve it, and gave His life blood for our salvation. Our love must extend to "sinners" and enemies. Luke writes in Luke 6:32, "If you love those who love you, what credit is that to you? Even 'sinners' love those who love them." It is not enough to say that we love others, although we must declare it, but we must also show it by our deeds and by caring for the needs that they have.

To whom do we communicate love? We should follow Jesus' example and show love, to all men! We must truly speak and manifest love to our own loved ones, including spouses and families, and brethren, as well as to those who oppose us, our "enemies", if we are to have genuine and victorious communication of the love God has given us.

The essence of all our Christian communication is that we must **communicate Jesus Christ.** John speaks of the proclamation of the Word, Jesus Christ, most relevantly in his first epistle. I John 1:1 clearly states his testimony, "That which was from the beginning, which we have heard, which we have seen with our eyes, which we have looked at and our hands have touched—this we proclaim concerning the Word of life."

This is the communication of the victory upon which our salvation rests. It is not based on hearsay or second hand information, but on the reality of John's own experience. When we declare the things that we have personally tasted from the Lord, there is an impact of victorious communication. Sharing our lives and our own experiences, joys, and victories brings a life giving testimony to others.

John expands his testimony of the reality of the Son of God dwelling with men in I John 1:2-3, "The life appeared; we have seen it and testify to it, and we proclaim to you the eternal life, which was with the Father and has appeared to us. We proclaim to you what we have seen and heard, so that you also may have fellowship with us. And our fellowship is with the Father and with his Son, Jesus Christ."

In *all we do* we must proclaim and communicate the Lord Jesus. What we have heard, seen, and touched we must proclaim out of pure hearts so that the hearers may go beyond survival to victory.

If we communicate victory, we will have that victory. If we communicate it in our families, we will have victorious families. If we communicate it in our churches, we will have victorious churches. If we speak it and show it in our lives, we can be victorious. If the little birds in the snow can sing a victorious song, we can sing our songs of victory day by day as we serve the Lord Jesus.

We will not communicate victory unless we commit to do so. When we only make promises that can be easily broken, we will reach survival but not victory. However, when we truly commit to communicate victory, and then seek diligently to keep our commitment, we will be victorious winners.

Mark—Seeing Beyond the Problems

As a pastor and righteous man, Mark saw problems, failures, and unrighteous lives every day. Because of this, his defenses rose up to challenge the spiritual sources that ravaged peoples lives. The battle went on and he regained ground that the enemy had taken from the people to whom he gave pastoral care. But something had happened to him in the process. He went about his labors with a heavy spirit. His wife and family were obviously living under the weight of his heavy spirit and words. Then something broke through to his spirit and he heard the sound of the grace of God. Things changed.

Mark began to see beyond the problems into the place of the victory that God had reserved for His children. He began communicating life and hope, victory and vision. Today his congregation and his family have a new look of joy and peace. As he continues to speak victory the church is growing and the city is reaping the benefits of the congregation's victory.

Summary of Part IV

In summary, we are communicating and will continue to communicate. The goal that we must pursue is to be victorious in and by our communications. Here are some of the primary thoughts that may be helpful to rehearse once more.

A. **We must communicate life, not death.** We will communicate one or the other. We have the option. We must choose life, and benefit others around us.

B. **We communicate by speaking.** Our words must be edifying and clear, so that we may be a blessing to others. Never withhold the declaration of God's will, purposes, and grace.

C. **We communicate by our gestures.** We must be careful to show His presence in our life even by our "body language".

D. **We communicate by our actions.** Remember that the things we do influence others, whether by blessing them or rejecting them. Be diligent and quick to respond to the needs of others.

E. **We communicate by our attitudes.** The ways that we respond or fail to respond to others can be a part of sowing righteousness leading to victory or leaving others unfulfilled and only able to survive.

F. **We must lay aside our selfish ways.** Resentment, unforgiveness, and unconfessed sins can taint our hearts so that our communication becomes corrupt and carries death to others. Let His will be predominant in our daily lives.

G. **We must rule our tongues and speak life.** Remember that the words that we speak can be spirit and life to those in need. Let us produce life in others by the life that we communicate.

H. **We must communicate faith, hope, and love.** These three elements live forever, and they edify and encourage all of us to victory in Jesus Christ.

I. **We must communicate Jesus Christ.** All things are in Him, by Him and nothing was made without Him. He is our life.

We must not permit Satan to rob us by speaking unbelief or despair, or worse yet by becoming sullen and silent. We have victory in our hearts and in our mouths! We can thrive, not just survive. The Apostle Paul declares in I Corinthians 15:57-58, "But thanks be to God! He gives us the victory through our Lord Jesus Christ. Therefore, my dear brothers, stand firm. Let nothing move you. Always give yourselves fully to the work of the Lord, because you know that your labor in the Lord is not in vain."

PART FIVE—FAITH

THE DOOR

*T*he final broad area that we must consider is faith. Faith really undergirds every thing else that we have considered. It indeed is the element that provides access to our eternal life in Jesus Christ. Faith brings us to emotional victory. Faith makes possible good relationships. Faith causes us to handle finances in a righteous manner. The words of faith we speak bring victory in our communications. Faith even pleases God, and lets us enjoy the salvation He has provided.

Have you seen a bush or plant that once flourished, but through hot, dry weather became wilted and unfruitful? Perhaps we look like that bush to the Lord Jesus. The once green leaves turn brown. The once pliable branches grow brittle. The roots do not find the water or the nutrition to cause blooming and fruitfulness. But somehow it lives. It survives.

There is life in the stalk and in the central clump of the root. This plant survives, but it is not pleasing to the gardener nor to the passerby in this condition. Yet that seed which started the growth in the first place still has a little life, although not a victorious, fruitful life.

If it maintains life until the rains come and water the earth, it can spring forth to a renewed strength and vigorous growth. The branches grow strong and flexible once again. New leaves appear and restore the freshness and beauty of the plant. There is victory and the promise of fruit and a harvest.

The once defeated Christian does have hope for victory. By faith we can see the goodness of the Lord in the land of the living. By faith we can overcome weeks, months, years, or decades of failures and mere survival. It is time for each of us to move from survival to victory in our faith and begin to please God and to become fruitful in Him.

The writer of Hebrews declares in Hebrews 11:6 "...without faith it is impossible to please God, because anyone who comes to him must believe that he exists and that he rewards those who earnestly seek him.(NIV).

One reason so many Christians fail to please God is that they have never attained to a victorious faith. A victorious faith seems to please everyone except the defeated Satan.

Paul echoes the prophetic voices from the Old Testament when he declares in Ephesians 2:8 "For it is by grace you have been saved, through faith—and this not from yourselves, it is the gift of God...." The quest for victorious faith is then not without reward. Such faith is an attainable goal. God, by His loving care and through His redeeming grace, has provided the faith that is required. He made it a free gift, so that man could not boast, and that makes it available to all of us.

How simple, yet how incomprehensible, is the favor that He has bestowed on us through our Lord Jesus Christ. To think that one so lowly as I could please the great Creator God is beyond my mind's ability to grasp. Yet that love which led our Savior to Calvary, has provided all things for all men through the gift of a minute seed of faith which He also provided. Both salvation faith and miracle working faith spring from that same seed.

The forces in the world around us tend to intimidate us when we rely on our own strength. We hear the cry from those without faith that there is "a lion in the street". The world's monetary dilemma causes worldly men to lose heart and hope. The threats of sickness, disease and inadequate medical care appear to be a judgment upon cultures and nations all around the world. Earthquakes, floods, forest fires, volcanoes, hurricanes, tornadoes, mud slides, ozone losses, global warming and every other conceivable ecological condition bring men without faith to a somber place of destitute attitudes. Contamination of rivers, oceans and even the very soil men walk on and live on seem to pose a threat to our children's futures.

With all these impending disasters seemingly about to fall upon us, it is understandable that a survival faith is all that many Christians can muster. *But* there is hope. We serve a mighty God who *never* lost a battle and who has made provision for our faith as well as our salvation.

In Habakkuk 3:17-19 we find that the prophet faced some similar difficult situations, but he faced them with a sound of victorious faith. "Though the fig tree does not bud and there are no grapes on the vines, though the olive crop fails and the fields produce no food, though there are no sheep in the pen and no cattle in the stalls, yet I will rejoice in the LORD, I will be joyful in God my Savior. The Sovereign LORD is my strength; he makes my feet like the feet of a deer, he enables me to go on the heights."(NIV)

We should remember that this is the same prophet that declared in

Habakkuk 2:4 "Behold, his soul which is lifted up is not upright in him: but the just shall live by his faith."(KJV).

Nathan—Stands in Faith

I have a precious friend, Nathan, in Kenya, who is a native pastor and spiritual leader to many people. He is a teacher to other native pastors and a leader of others who teach and evangelize the people of Kenya and the surrounding countries. He has been beaten and robbed more than once. He has had his property destroyed, and been rejected by men. But Nathan stands in faith.

Men who beat him and robbed him have afterward come to him asking if he would teach them how to become Christians. They saw how he endured in his faith, even while he was being persecuted, and also read the literature they stole from him which he used in teaching. God brought the persecuters to salvation. Many native ministers come to Nathan to learn how to teach the Gospel and how Christians should live, so that they might teach others. He, and others that labor with him are living expressions of the Book of Acts. Nathan has found the door to faith and victory in Jesus Christ.

It appears obvious that victory in our faith does not come out of our circumstances, no matter what they might be, but comes from trusting what God says more than the reports coming from the world around us. Our faith is in the faithful God who has redeemed us through His own Son and walks with us and in us by the Holy Spirit which He has given to us. Faith is the door that leads to overcoming victory in every aspect of our lives.

I Peter 1:3-9 deals with overcoming condemnation by our lively hope and by confirmation and assurance of our salvation. The Apostle Peter writes, "Praise be to the God and Father of our Lord Jesus Christ! In his great mercy he has given us new birth into a living hope through the resurrection of Jesus Christ from the dead, and into an inheritance that can never perish, spoil or fade—kept in heaven for you, who through faith are shielded by God's power until the coming of the salvation that is ready to be revealed in the last time. In this you greatly rejoice, though now for a little while you may have had to suffer grief in all kinds of trials. These have come so that your faith—of greater worth than gold, which perishes even though refined by fire—may be proved genuine and may result in praise, glory and honor when Jesus Christ is revealed. Though you have not seen him, you love him; and even though you do not see him now, you believe in him and are filled with an inexpressible and glorious joy, for you are receiving the goal of your faith, the salvation of your souls." (NIV)

CHAPTER TWENTY THREE

CONDEMNATION

*C*ondemnation was the first fruit of Adam's sin of disobedience in the Garden of Eden. When he ate of the fruit of the tree of the knowledge of good and evil, he recognized his own nakedness and tried to hide from God. Ever since that fateful day, unregenerate men feel condemnation when God is present, and they will continue to attempt to hide until a greater day comes. That greater day is the day that we accept, acknowledge, and receive the release from all sin through faith in the Lord Jesus Christ.

We read one of the most often cited of all Bible stories in John 8:3-11, "The teachers of the law and the Pharisees brought in a woman caught in adultery. They made her stand before the group and said to Jesus, 'Teacher, this woman was caught in the act of adultery. In the Law Moses commanded us to stone such women. Now what do you say?' They were using this question as a trap, in order to have a basis for accusing him. But Jesus bent down and started to write on the ground with his finger. When they kept on questioning him, he straightened up and said to them, 'If any one of you is without sin, let him be the first to throw a stone at her.' Again he stooped down and wrote on the ground. At this, those who heard began to go away one at a time, the older ones first, until only Jesus was left, with the woman still standing there. Jesus straightened up and asked her, 'Woman, where are they? Has no one condemned you?' 'No one, sir,' she said. 'Then neither do I condemn you,' Jesus declared. 'Go now and leave your life of sin.'" (NIV)

What can negate our faith more quickly and more completely than the immediately impending threat of death? This woman was utterly without hope. She was guilty, captive, and condemned. Both the law of Moses and her own conscience said that she was in sin and worthy of execution. The men who brought her to Jesus were merciless and eager to both stone her and to catch Jesus in some violation of their laws and customs. The trap was set and there seemed to be no room for faith in God to offer mercy and grace to redeem her from condemnation. Yet, Jesus did just that. He removed the threat of men. He forgave her of her sin. He turned her life, headed toward death, into a life filled with the faith that overcomes hell and the grave.

The same condemnation that rested on this woman tends to oppress everyone who sins or who even makes a small mistake. There are certainly degrees, or levels, of condemnation depending on the individual's concept of the magnitude of his failure or sin. Yet, we find that even a small measure of condemnation can cause a righteous man to fail to have the faith that all of us so drastically need in our walk with God.

Condemnation and failure to appropriate God's love and grace cause many of His children to suffer great anguish. Agreement with the accusations of Satan and surrender to the vain imaginations of our own minds can devastate and render useless the Christian who is under the attack of condemnation.

This spirit of condemnation is not a new device to alienate men from God. It is as old as sin. In the garden of Eden when Adam and Eve ate the forbidden fruit, condemnation came to separate them from God. When God called to the man, "Where are you?", Adam responded, "I heard thy voice in the garden, and I was afraid, because I was naked; and I hid myself." Condemnation and guilt were there because of sin, but faith and grace had not yet entered the domain of man's experience and understanding.

How often our actions and even our thoughts cause us to hide from the loving father. Adam's fall has left us with the stamp of sin and condemnation, and the first reaction of our flesh is to stand condemned rather than to cry out to the Lord Jesus who has provided deliverance for us from the weight of condemnation by His own sacrifice on Calvary. We now have an advocate with the Father. When our faith reaches up to Him every condemning, Pharisaical accuser must back away as Jesus writes on the soil from which we were made as earthy, human creatures, yet somehow in the likeness of the Creator.

When the Lord Jesus enters the picture everything changes just as it did for the adulterous, condemned woman. Light and grace shine into our hearts as the heavy load of sin is transferred from our shoulders to the loving Savior who already bore all our sins on Mt. Calvary. Victory, instead of mere survival, results as we see our selves as God sees us: redeemed and sinless.

Satan and his worldly cohorts are not pleased when we walk in victory, but the option to walk in victory by faith has been given into our hands. There are two levels where our faith must rise up and claim our victory so that we can please God. The first of these is salvation faith, and the second is functional faith that moves mountains and brings miracles.

In Romans 8:1-2 Paul encourages us by saying, "There is therefore now no condemnation to them which are in Christ Jesus, who walk not after the flesh, but after the Spirit. For the law of the Spirit of life in Christ Jesus hath made me free from the law of sin and death." Paul's explanation which follows in the next two verses is that sin in the flesh has been condemned, but that we are made free as we walk in the spirit by faith and by His grace which gives that faith. He cites the weakness of the law because of the flesh, and the righteousness which has been fulfilled through Jesus the Son of God.

This is the foundation of our salvation faith, yet many forget, or even doubt, that this deliverance from condemnation applies to them. How often we see those who have known the Lord Jesus for years feeling anxious for their own salvation. From time to time we counsel with people who say, "I don't know," when asked where they stand regarding their salvation. These are frequently people who have been going to church for years, and apparently doing all the things that are expected of them.

This is not as God intended it to be. By faith, we must rise up and believe the Scriptures. God wants you to just agree with His Word. He has provided; we need only to stand in faith and rejoice in the provision that He has made. This is victory over condemnation. If we have sins that bring the condemnation, repentance is certainly in order, but after we have sincerely repented, we have only to believe by faith. Remember that whoever comes to Him he will not reject or cast aside. I John 1:9 tells us, "If we confess our sins, he is faithful and just and will forgive us our sins and purify us from all unrighteousness." (NIV) The Father loves His children.

The second area of faith which is rendered ineffective by condemnation is functional faith. By this we mean the faith which causes us to be able to fulfill the callings and giftings that God has put into our lives. This is the faith that permits the operation of spiritual gifts in our lives. This is the faith that gives us boldness to be witnesses and to testify to others of the grace that He has given to us and for them. Functional faith makes us victorious in our daily activities, as well as in the times of great stress and trials which we all will face as we grow in Christ.

Condemnation blights our ability to respond in boldness to the workings of the Spirit through us. Paul admonished Timothy in II Timothy 1:7-8, "For God did not give us a spirit of timidity, but a spirit of power, of love and of self-discipline. So do not be ashamed to testify about our Lord, or ashamed of me his prisoner. But join with me in suffering for the gospel, by the power of God". (NIV)

When we stand condemned by our own thoughts or actions, that power, love and self-discipline are negated, and we find ourselves ashamed of the Gospel and of ourselves. When we recognize the great truth of our release from condemnation, we can do all things through Christ who strengthens us. We must have functional faith to enter and labor in the Kingdom of God which is composed of righteousness, peace and joy in the Holy Spirit.

Oliver—Overcoming Condemnation

Oliver has been a dedicated Christian since his college days. He always desired to fulfill the call that God put into his life, but never seemed to feel adequate to do what he felt that he was supposed to do. This yearning to please God never left him, but the realization of the goal always eluded him. God was constantly there for him, and that consistency kept drawing Oliver to seek His will. However, the frustration of feelings of failure was reflected in his family and in his personal attitudes toward everything in his daily life.

Finally he sought out spiritual help to learn how to overcome condemnation and rise up to victory. It was hard at first, but as he heard words of faith, he began to appropriate faith for himself. In one particular gathering where God was moving and faith ran high, Oliver made a giant step toward active, functioning faith to do as well as hear God's Word. From that moment a change began in him that is still taking place. His family reflects the faith that has come alive in him, and he is growing in the ministries that God has had for him all these years. His wife and children are also manifesting a new joy as Oliver operates in this new level of faith. God has once again responded to man's cry of faith.

Let us examine ourselves diligently to detect any traces of condemnation that may attempt to defeat us. He will wash us, strengthen us, and help us to be fruitful servants. Peter tells us that the Father has caused us to be born again to a living hope through the resurrection of Jesus Christ. Let us walk in that resurrection life and fulfill every gifting and calling He has given us.

"Thanks be to God! He gives us the victory through our Lord Jesus Christ." (I Cor.15:57) (NIV)

CHAPTER TWENTY FOUR

CONTEMPLATION

*M*uch of our faith, or lack of faith, is based on paradigms from our own mental processes. To the Lord Jesus a little child epitomized the Kingdom of God. He said that unless we become like a little child we do not have access to the Kingdom. Small children have not acquired mind-sets that block their faith, and therefore they are trusting and faithful. We are, however, not little children.

In I Corinthians 14:20 Paul said, "Brothers, stop thinking like children. In regard to evil be infants, but in your thinking be adults."(NIV) Our innocence regarding evil, malice, distrust and other divisive elements is required by the Lord Jesus if we are to please Him and enter His Kingdom. Yet, we are to be mature in our thinking if we are to be productive citizens of that Kingdom.

Our thoughts can defeat us if we are not wise. Galatians 6:3 tells us, "If anyone thinks he is something when he is nothing, he deceives himself."(NIV) Vain imaginations about ourselves, can be delusive and yield disastrous misconceptions. Faith and presumption are not synonyms. If we look closely, we will find that presumption usually emerges from personal desires for success in some area. Whether these desire are for good, neutral, or bad things, the assumption that God will honor our own motives can be deceptive and cause defeat.

It is important that we recognize presumption for what it is, and in turn move to a faith that is in agreement with the Word of God. When we let our minds be ruled by self seeking motives we court disaster, but there is a way to have God's wisdom in our considerations.

The apostle James has valuable instruction as to how we can obtain the wisdom that brings stability. James 1:5-8 reads, "If any of you lacks wisdom, he should ask God, who gives generously to all without finding fault, and it will be given to him. But when he asks, he must believe and not doubt, because he who doubts is like a wave of the sea, blown and tossed by the wind. That man should not think he will receive anything from the Lord; he is a double-minded man, unstable in all he does."(NIV)

God's gracious provisions are available to us when we ask of Him, even to the granting of wisdom which overcomes presumption. Single-mindedness is obviously an attribute which brings stability, and this comes by having a faith that does not doubt. This is all in the realm of our thoughts; the battleground of our faith.

In the eighth chapter of Romans, verses 6 and 7, we are taught that if we are carnally minded the fruit is death but if we are spiritually minded we reap life and peace. Further we are told that the carnal mind is enmity against God. Again it becomes obvious that we must be spiritual, if we are to exercise faith, but the determination of that spiritual position is found in our minds. How easy it is to see that we must bring every thought into captivity.

When Jesus delivered the man of the Gerasenes from the legion of demons that possessed him, the people saw the sign of his healing in the fact that he was clothed and "in his right mind." This man became a righteous witness to his city of what God had done for him. The mind that has encountered Christ is the victorious mind and manifests faith that is persuasive to the hearers. It is the mind that can drive back the darkness of oppression. It is the mind that can see things clearly and choose righteousness. It is the mind that speaks strength to the weak and health to the afflicted.

The men who reject God in their minds and knowledge are those whom God gives over to what is referred to in Romans 1:28 as a "reprobate" mind. Webster's definition of reprobate is "rejected as worthless, not standing a test, condemned, foreordained to damnation, morally abandoned, or depraved." This is, indeed, an extremely undesirable state. In Romans 1:29-31 we find the results that a reprobate mind yield in such an individual. This list includes wickedness, evil, greed, depravity, envy, murder, strife, deceit, malice, gossip, and slander. It further states that they are God-haters, insolent, arrogant and boastful; they invent ways of doing evil; they disobey their parents; they are senseless, faithless, heartless, ruthless. All of this results from rejecting God in their minds and understanding.

Since the mind is the battleground of our faith, we can see that we must seek and receive Him if we are to win the war. We contemplate many things every day. We plan our futures. We consider our relationships and finances. We permit our thoughts to lead us into either emotional victories or defeats. But there is a glorious victory for all who look in the right direction and permit God to be the center of our contemplation.

Patrick—A New Perspective From Another Land

Patrick had been injured, in his spirit not his body. He felt as though his wounds had left him abandoned and inadequate, incompetent and inept. A degree of bitterness was in him although he tried to disguise it even from himself. He still functioned as a spiritual leader in his church, but the freshness and jubilation that should be present in spiritual things was not in evidence. There was a stalemate which relied on patterns of behavior rather than the life of the Holy Spirit.

Although many friends tried to help him out of this survivalist mode, God had to sovereignly move on him to restore him to his first love and the faith to overcome the enemy of our souls. A short-term missions trip provided the impetus to bring Patrick back to the faith and purpose that was his. He saw the real needs of the downtrodden people of another land and got new perspective. He also saw the tremendous response to the Gospel among the spiritually destitute and realized that God had equipped him to serve those needs.It did not take long before He was victorious again in the Spirit and by faith he was reclaiming the years that had been stolen from him. Today he is like a fruitful vine full of good works in the Kingdom of God.

Paul gives us a truth in Romans that is the essence of our mind's victory. Romans 12:2 instructs us, "Do not conform any longer to the pattern of this world, but be transformed by the renewing of your mind. Then you will be able to test and approve what God's will is—his good, pleasing and perfect will."(NIV)

As we examine this verse, we learn the way to find the will of God. How often do Christians ask "what is the will of God" for one problem after another? We find it through removing our minds from the world's concepts and precepts, and having minds that are changed and enlightened by the Holy Spirit. Without this renewing we would fail to recognize the pure will of God, even if it were spoken prophetically by His servants.

Once we undergo this change, we can make righteous judgements. Paul tells us that we have "the mind of Christ", if we are spiritual, and that we can judge all things (I Corinthians 2:15). However, to walk in this "mind of Christ" is a transformation process that we learn as we grow in Him. When we are born of the Spirit, everything that we need for our Christian walk is made accessible to us, but like a baby learning to crawl, then walk, then run, we must grow. At first we need milk in the process. Later we can have strong meat. If we persevere, we can have renewed minds and truly prove His good, pleasing and perfect will.

In Philippians we find a most insightful Scripture drawing a picture of the true mind of the Lord Jesus in His mission for our salvation. Here in the second chapter Paul tells us to be "likeminded", to have the same love, to be of one accord and one mind. Here our mind's attitudes can come to be tested. He speaks of that lowliness of mind which enables us to esteem everyone else better than ourselves. He teaches us to abandon strife and vainglory. He paints a portrait of men who care for the welfare of others ahead of themselves. These are the "likeminded" men. At this juncture we can hear the ultimate in having the mind of Christ as Paul portrays the God-Man's own mind through recounting His actions.

Philippians 2:5-8 reads, "Let this mind be in you, which was also in Christ Jesus: Who, being in the form of God, thought it not robbery to be equal with God: But made himself of no reputation, and took upon him the form of a servant, and was made in the likeness of men: And being found in fashion as a man, he humbled himself, and became obedient unto death, even the death of the cross."(KJV)

What is our mind-set? How do we comprehend this drastic example that is set before us? With renewed minds we have the victory that removes us from the struggling, almost defeated survival mode of the world around us, and we move into the place of overcoming faith where His example is our pattern and our joy. Setting aside the world's attitudes as unprofitable, we find the joy and victory that comes in emulating Him in all things even unto that willingness to lay down our lives for Christ and for one another.

This, however, is not the end of the story. In Philipians 2 we find the real, eternal results of the renewed mind and the resultant laid down life. Here God steps in on His behalf and on behalf of all those who follow Him. Here is our victory.

Philippians 2:9-11 gives us the glorious results, "Therefore God exalted him to the highest place and gave him the name that is above every name, that at the name of Jesus every knee should bow, in heaven and on earth and under the earth, and every tongue confess that Jesus Christ is Lord, to the glory of God the Father." (NIV)

CHAPTER TWENTY FIVE

CONFIRMATION

*J*oshua 1:6-9 gives us this word of encouragement, "Be strong and courageous, because you will lead these people to inherit the land I swore to their forefathers to give them. Be strong and very courageous. Be careful to obey all the law my servant Moses gave you; do not turn from it to the right or to the left, that you may be successful wherever you go. Do not let this Book of the Law depart from your mouth; meditate on it day and night, so that you may be careful to do everything written in it. Then you will be prosperous and successful. Have I not commanded you? Be strong and courageous. Do not be terrified; do not be discouraged, for the LORD your God will be with you wherever you go." (NIV)

Faith is positive! It does not yield to fear. It does not faint in the times of great opposition and discouraging circumstances. Faith does not settle for survival. Faith always claims a victorious outcome, even in the face of the overwhelming presence of the adversary of our souls. Faith gives us the victory that overcomes the world. Faith is active, vision inspiring, and brings joy to all who embrace it.

How do we get faith? Faith comes by hearing, and hearing comes by the Word of God, according to Romans 10:17. Although faith is a gift from God, we need the hearing ears that let faith take root and grow within us. A little seed of faith grows into a great victory as we nurture and exercise it. Survival turns to "thrival" as we thrive in the garden of faith where the Word of God is planted in our hearts and minds.

How do we reach our victory in the realm of faith? How do we open the faith door that gives us victory in all aspects of our Christian walk? How do we keep the victory over Satan's attacks against us by his temptations, accusations, and condemnations? How can we consistently rule our meditations and the contemplation of the many sounds and voices that continually come against the profession of our faith?

James 2:17-20 tells us, "In the same way, faith by itself, if it is not accompanied by action, is dead. But someone will say, 'You have faith; I have deeds.' Show me your faith without deeds, and I will show you my faith by what I do. You believe that there is one God. Good! Even the demons believe that—and shudder. You foolish man, do you want evidence that faith without deeds is useless?" (NIV)

Our faith is confirmed to others, to ourselves, and to God by our actions.

Just as a lamp with its light bulb must have the electrical current flowing to it to light a room, so the expression of our faith must have our actions to bring light and victory to our Christian walk. The active electrical current causes the filament of the bulb to glow to produce the light. The light of our actions confirms the presence of the current of faith.

However, if the bulb is dead, or burned out, the current will not cause it to glow. When there is no manifestation of light, we can't be sure that the current is really there. So faith, without action or works of some sort, is ineffective if it is indeed present at all. When we are truly filled with faith, we will show it by our actions, behavior, and attitudes.

When the Lord Jesus calls out to us across the waters, we must have the faith to get out of the boat if we are to walk with Him on the waves. Even then there are times when we need His hand to lift us so that we don't sink and have to resort to swimming to survive. Survival by swimming with our fleshly strength is typical of the life that many Christians lead today. Victory comes, however, as we clearly hear His call, know His voice, and set out by faith to go to Him and do the works that He has given us to do.

Although we must not fear stepping out in faith, we must guard against mistaking presumption for faith. Presumption is rooted in the carnal mind. Faith is rooted in God's word.

Presumption is usually generated by listening to the voice of our own desires and ambitions. Faith is generated by His voice, His word to us, which is confirmed by conformity to scriptural principles.

Presumption rushes ahead of God's timing. This is always a hazard when we fail to hear God's word to us or when we permit our own desires to preempt His will. Presumption frequently becomes an alternative to obedience, but it can never become a viable substitute for faith.

The 11th chapter of Hebrews tells us that faith is the substance, or assurance, of our hopes, and is evidence of things which are not yet visible. It also presents the truth that all things that we now see were not made of visible matter. Many scientists have reached this same conclusion in the past few years by both investigation of the outer expanse of the universe and by computer calculations using data available to them.

The writer of Hebrews confirms His substance and evidence assessment of faith by citing the actions which came out of the reservoir of faith vested in biblical heroes of the Old Testament. He speaks of Enoch's walking with God and being "taken up" so that he did not taste death. He speaks of the actions which resulted from Abraham's faith and the sacrifices that men made by faith which pleased God. He speaks of obedience performed, persecutions suffered, and victories won through the manifestations of active faith. All these historical accounts teach and inspire us, but the conclusion after all these glorious victories is that our portion is a better provision from God because we have Jesus Christ as both author and finisher of our faith. He set the example, and He provides the victory.

Our victory comes as we risk *all* in this life by trusting in Him. We usually only risk the things that men value highly in this life, these things ultimately only bring survival. What appears to be great risk in the eyes of men is not really a risk of anything eternal. Men risk much to become successful, or full of success. We risk what we risk to become faithful, or full of faith. The result is that we live by the faith of the Son of God who loved and died for us. The Christ of all faith lives in us as surely as we dwell in these earthly, physical bodies.

Rita—A Woman of Faith

The greatest confirmations of the results of our faith do not necessarily come to theologians or great preachers. Rita was a steady, faithful Christian mother and housewife. She helped and blessed others, but did not have the outward confirmation of the faith that was potentially hers. A series of attacks against her family, including a life threatening illness to one of her children, served to raise her up to become a woman of faith who could stand against Satan, fight the good fight of faith, and win the victory over every circumstance. She became strong in the times of her greatest trials.

Today Rita has a renewed mind that will not give place to the enemy. She has a walk of faith that attests to the victory in her heart. She may never go to foreign lands to convert unbelievers, but she will win many victories among those around her where she lives every day.

The victories overcome the survival mode as our active faith comes to fullness in us because of His Presence and His faithfulness. The requirement is that we trust in Him and His Word to taste the sweet rewards of victory.

Every practical victory in this life is ours by faith. We have been given that faith which comes down as a good and perfect gift from the Father. Here are some of the victories that are ours by faith.

A. **By faith we can overcome condemnation** and trust the Lord Jesus and His Word in every aspect of our lives.

B. **By faith we can be active, fruitful doers of the Word** and see the results of His victory in our efforts in the Church which is His Body.

C. **By faith we can walk in a consistent relationship with our Lord Jesus.** With His assurance, His love, and His salvation we can become glowing examples of the righteousness, peace, and joy that we share in His Kingdom.

D. **By faith we can acknowledge that He is our ever present help** in times of trouble, and recognize that He is the One who never lost a battle.

E. **By faith we can overcome Satan** and all the demonic forces that he sends against those who belong to Jesus Christ. He does not have dominion over us, but we have been given authority over him by the blood of our Lord Jesus.

F. **By faith we can reverse the old patterns** of criticism and conflict in our relationships in the church and in the world around us, and fulfill Jesus' instructions for living in the Kingdom of God as stated in the 6th chapter of Luke's gospel.

G. **By faith we can function in the gifts and callings** that God has put into our lives, and thus benefit and edify ourselves, our brothers and sisters in Christ, and the unredeemed in the world around us.

H. **By faith we can see the goodness of the Lord right now** in the land of the living. Christians have put off until "tomorrow" all the riches and victories of the Kingdom of God for far too long. Let us use the faith He has given for victory now!

In I John 5:4-5 we find a concise word which we can all appropriate for our own victory. He says, "for everyone born of God overcomes the world. This is the victory that has overcome the world, even our faith. Who is it that overcomes the world? Only he who believes that Jesus is the Son of God."

THE CONCLUSION IS VICTORY

*T*he Apostle Paul drew a conclusion in I Corinthians 15:54 which summarizes all our hopes for the future. He declares, "When the perishable has been clothed with the imperishable, and the mortal with immortality, then the saying that is written will come true: 'Death has been swallowed up in victory.'"

This passage is a clear promise of ultimate victory for all believers. Yet this same faith brings victory all along the way as we walk in Christ. The five primary areas that we have dealt with in these chapters really directly or indirectly encompass all the practical activities of our daily lives. None of the seemingly formidable problems can steal our victory if we can walk with Christ daily.

Prayer is certainly a key function in every aspect of our life in Christ. It is necessary if we are to both hear and do the things which we have discussed and which lead from survival to victory every day. Yet even in prayer we must avoid mere survival and claim the victory that we have in Him.

As I ministered in a church recently, a word of exhortation and vision was spoken which was directly applicable to that local church. As I considered it later, I realized that it had a broader application that applies to all of us as part of the active, living church of the Lord Jesus Christ in this day. I would like to share a paraphrase of that word with all who read this, to exhort and encourage all of us to go forward to the work at hand.

First of all, we must recognize that we are all where we are for God's purposes and in accordance with His plans. He would have all of us to grow to a new stature in Him. We are being changed to conform to the image of Christ.

We are where we are so that we can be prepared for the works of service to which we are appointed. The fullness of the stature of Christ can only be attained as individual members become what He intends for each of us to be.

All of us must reach out to the people around us. The harvest is ripe and God is hiring laborers. Our commission as witnesses cannot be ignored.

We must also recognize that we have been recruited into service so that the areas beyond where we live may also hear the Gospel and be discipled in Jesus Christ. Matthew 28:19-20 continues to give a clarion call to all who will hear it.

These words were very real to me in their original context. I hope they will be real to all of us, as we are all appointed to accomplish His mission. The assignment to the church to care for those who are in need must be fulfilled. As we bless those who need very practical help, we begin to do the will of God as expressed in so many scriptures. As we read Isaiah 58:6-12, we hear the sound of God's heart toward the oppressed, the hungry, and the homeless and naked, and we find the promises of victory which accrue to those who obey.

If we the church are to do the things which we hear by the spirit, we need victory in the areas of emotions, relationships, finances, communications, and faith. Hopefully the insights and admonitions presented in the earlier chapters will bring all of us to victory in these areas.

The prophet Zephaniah paints a vivid picture of the people who, though afflicted and poor, attain righteousness and win great victory and find themselves redeemed and in the presence of the Lord God. May we all enjoy this same victory.

The Lord declares in Zephaniah 3:12-17, "But I will leave within you the meek and humble, who trust in the name of the LORD. The remnant of Israel will do no wrong; they will speak no lies, nor will deceit be found in their mouths. They will eat and lie down and no one will make them afraid. Sing, O Daughter of Zion; shout aloud, O Israel! Be glad and rejoice with all your heart, O Daughter of Jerusalem! The LORD has taken away your punishment, he has turned back your enemy. The LORD, the King of Israel, is with you; never again will you fear any harm. On that day they will say to Jerusalem, 'Do not fear, O Zion; do not let your hands hang limp. The LORD your God is with you, he is mighty to save. He will take great delight in you, he will quiet you with his love, he will rejoice over you with singing.'" (NIV)